SCRIPTURE AND THE CHARISMATIC RENEWAL

Scripture and the Charismatic Renewal

Proceedings of
the Milwaukee Symposium
December 1–3, 1978

Edited by
George Martin

SERVANT BOOKS
Ann Arbor, Michigan

Published by Servant Books
        Box 8617
        Ann Arbor, Michigan 48107

Printed in the United States of America

ISBN 0-89283-070-0

Contents

Contributors

Avery Dulles, S.J., is a professor of theology at the Catholic University of America, in Washington, D.C.

Paul Hinnebusch, O.P., is a well-known author and retreat master and currently lives in Dallas, Texas.

William S. Kurz, S.J., teaches scripture at Marquette University, in Milwaukee, Wisconsin.

George Martin, the editor for this volume, received a doctorate in philosophy from the University of Notre Dame.

George Montague, S.M., is president of the Catholic Biblical Association and teaches at the University of St. Michael's College, in Toronto, Canada.

James A. O'Brien is the director of the Upper Room Spiritual Center, New Monmouth, New Jersey.

INTRODUCTION

The Bible is assuming a role of increasing importance in the Catholic Church. Despite accusations to the contrary, the Catholic Church has never forgotten its scriptural heritage, though admittedly there has sometimes been a neglect of the Bible on the part of many Catholics. The Second Vatican Council reaffirmed beyond all doubt the place of scripture in the Church and encouraged Catholics to read the Bible as God's word. The liturgical renewal stemming from Vatican II has brought scripture into the lives of Catholics in a concrete way by means of the new lectionary readings.

Two other developments have greatly affected the role that scripture has played in the Catholic Church in the last decades. First, Pius XII's 1943 encyclical *Divino Afflante Spiritu* provided the much-needed impetus for the development of mature Catholic scripture scholarship. Second, the Catholic charismatic renewal has sparked an ever-growing, popular movement of scripture reading among Catholics. Never before have so many ordinary Catholics turned to the Bible to nourish their faith and so many Catholic scholars been involved with the work of exegesis.

However, the gap between the scholar's understanding of scripture and the popular reading of the Bible by Catholics is often considerable. At its extreme, some of the conclusions reached by scholars employing the historical-critical method would scandalize the faith of most Catholics, and the popular understanding of scripture held by many Catholics would be dismissed as naive by scholars. Even without focusing on the extremes of this gap, it is clear that much of the fruit of Catholic scripture scholarship has yet to be tasted by the ordinary Catholic.

Many scholars have been disturbed by what they perceive as a tendency to biblical fundamentalism among those who ap-

1

proach scripture without specific exegetical training. On the other hand, many ordinary Catholics have been inclined to distrust the scholarly approach to scripture, particularly when topics like the historicity of the gospels or the reality of miracles are treated as points of debate rather than matters of faith. Cardinal Suenens addressed these concerns in the first Malines Document.

> While the problems inherent in a fundamentalistic interpretation of the Bible should not be minimized, they should also not be exaggerated. What is seen by some as fundamentalism might not be fundamentalism at all. Many recent exegetes have seen the healings of Jesus as symbols, without reference to any historic healing event. When lay persons without exegetical training interpret these events as historically true, their literalism is not fundamentalistic. This also suggests that professional exegesis is best based on both faith-experience and scientific skills. (Cardinal Suenens, *Theological and Pastoral Orientations on the Catholic Charismatic Renewal* [Ann Arbor, Mich.: Servant Books, 1974], p. 40.)

No doubt, a certain amount of tension between those who take an analytical approach to scripture and those whose approach is more devotional and personal will always exist. But there is no reason to believe that ordinary Catholics cannot appropriate the insights of sound scholarship or that biblical scholars cannot respect the validity of personal, faith-filled reading of scripture.

Because participation in the charismatic renewal stimulates Catholics to read scripture, the use and understanding of scripture in the Catholic charismatic renewal is of some importance. In order to examine the theological and pastoral issues concerning the use of scripture in the charismatic renewal, a symposium was held in Milwaukee, December 1–3, 1978. Sponsored by the Steering Committee of the Diocesan Liaisons to the charismatic renewal, a body of those appointed to serve as liaisons between Roman Catholic bishops and the charismatic renewal in their dioceses, the symposium took a first step in formulating practical pastoral conclusions. Professional exegetes and theologians, pastoral leaders within the charismatic renewal, and diocesan liaisons sat down together to share reflections and insights from their own background and experience. The papers prepared for the symposium had been distributed in advance, and the symposium itself consisted of group interaction over the papers.

The four papers presented at the symposium were written by Avery Dulles, William Kurz, Paul Hinnebusch, and George Montague. After the completion of the symposium, James O'Brien drew together some of the considerations and conclusions of the discussions in order to present a profile of the symposium.

Avery Dulles' "The Bible in the Church: Some Debated Questions" summarizes the position of many contemporary Catholic theologians regarding the relationship between the Bible and the Church. To deal adequately with the complexities of this relationship, he takes a dialectical approach to such matters as the Church's role in formulating the canon, the Old Testament as preparation for the New, interpretation as a function of community, and the role of the Church's *magisterium* in interpreting the scripture.

In his paper "Inspiration and the Origins of the New Testament" William Kurz points out that Vatican II's *Dogmatic Constitution on Divine Revelation* has wide-ranging implications for interpreting scripture as both fully human and fully divine. He specifically considers the implications of the Council's teaching and the New Testament evidence that the divinely inspired word is mediated through the words of men and consequently is influenced by historical, cultural, and cognitive limitations.

Taken as a whole, the papers and conclusions of the symposium have application beyond the boundaries of the charismatic renewal. As Cardinal Suenens has noted:

> The manner in which lay people in the renewal approach the text does not differ from the manner in which the general lay population of the Church approaches the biblical text....

3

The difference is to be found in the role the reading of the Bible plays in the renewal as distinct from that within the general Catholic population. While this general Catholic population is not characterized by the great attention it accords to the scriptures as a major source of its spiritual food, great attention to the scriptures does typify the renewal. Suenens *Theological and Pastoral Orientations*, p.39–40.)

As more and more lay Catholics begin to read and study scripture, many of the concerns and pastoral recommendations raised by this symposium will have increasing significance for the Church.

George Martin

THE BIBLE IN THE CHURCH: SOME DEBATED QUESTIONS

Avery Dulles, S.J.

Since the early nineteenth century, when F. C. Baur and J. A. Möhler debated the question, many authors have tried to express in a single formula the fundamental difference between Catholic and Protestant Christianity. Not infrequently it is said that the Protestant comes to the Bible first, and to the Church second, whereas the Catholic goes through the Church as the more immediate guide, and then to the Bible. Catholics commonly appeal to the saying of Augustine, "I would not believe the Bible unless the authority of the Catholic Church moved me to do so."[1] Protestants, on the other hand, gravitate toward the position articulated in extreme form by William Chillingworth: "The Bible, I say, the Bible only, is the Religion of Protestants."[2] Although Protestants and Catholics have come much closer to agreement on many matters in the past generation, Vatican II remarked that they still differ in their views on the relationship between the Bible and the Church. In the Decree on Ecumenism, no. 21, we read:

> But when Christians separated from us affirm the divine authority of the sacred Books, they think differently from us—different ones in different ways—about the relationship between the Scriptures and the Church. In the Church, according to Catholic belief, an authentic teaching office plays a special role in the explanation and proclamation of the written word of God.

Nevertheless, in dialogue itself, the sacred utterances are precious instruments in the mighty hand of God for attaining that unity which the Savior holds out to all men.[3]

In general terms, we may say that Catholics continue to insist that the Bible is the Church's book and that it must be read and interpreted in the Church, with due reverence for Catholic tradition and for the Church's official teaching body (*magisterium*). Yet there is increasing recognition of the primacy and immediacy of the believer's contact with the Bible.

In the present paper I shall try to summarize what I would take to be the position of many contemporary Catholic theologians regarding the relationship between the Bible and the Church. I shall maintain that the relationship is a highly complex one, involving a dialectic of mutual priorities. It would be an oversimplification to hold either that the Church is prior to the Bible or that the Bible is prior to the Church. In order to stress the complexity of the relationship, I shall set forth my position in terms of ten propositions, each of which may be read with or without the particle *not*.

The Church did (not) write the Bible

When I was a student of theology, I had a professor who held, perhaps with deliberate exaggeration, that the Church did not really need the Bible, because God's revelation was in the Church's consciousness even before the scriptures were written. The Church today uses the scriptures as a means of teaching its own message, and it can so use them because the scriptures express the faith of the Church. If the scriptures were lost, it would make no great difference. The Church could write a new Bible by simply expressing its faith in written form.

While admitting some exaggeration in this position, we can rightly assert that the Bible emanates from the Church. This is particularly evident for the New Testament, which the Protestant exegete Willi Marxsen quite cheerfully characterizes as "the work of the Church."[4] The New Testament was in its entirety written by Christian churchmen. As Karl Rahner explains, rather fully, in his *Inspiration in the Bible*, the inspiration of the New Testament consists in its being a pure expression of the faith of the apostolic Church.[5] The individual authors were not simply expressing their private opinions but the Church's faith, and their writings have been received into the canon because they are seen as embodying that faith. Thus it may be said that the New Testament is an expression of the faith of the apostolic church, which wrote it.

The Old Testament was received, not written, by the Church. But still it was, in its origins, an ecclesial book. It expresses the faith of the people of God at a prior stage in the course of its formation. Insofar as ancient Israel was already a *gahal* (an assembly convoked by God), it may be called *church* in an extended sense of the term. For this reason and also because Christians looked upon the history of ancient Israel as the Church's own divinely intended prehistory, the Church regarded the Hebrew scriptures as ecclesial writings. In accepting these writings as its Old Testament, the Christian Church placed the Hebrew Bible in a new framework, and enabled it to be read and used as a vehicle of Christian faith. Thus the Old Testament, as part of the Christian Bible, in some sense derives from the Church, though not directly, as does the New Testament.

But as the negative form of my proposition asserts, there is a sense in which the Church did *not* write the Bible. The Bible is the word of God, and as such it is God's gift to the Church. Although the writers of the Old and New Testament belonged to a believing community of faith, and gave expression to the faith of their community, they did so by a special grace or charism, known as inspiration. In some cases the inspiration of the biblical writer coincided with a gift of prophecy (Isaiah, the seer of the Apocalypse,), in some cases with apostleship (Paul), in some cases with gifts of wisdom (the sapiential literature) or poetic creation (Psalms). In other instances inspiration took the form of an impulse and endowment for composing sacred history (Kings and Luke). Biblical inspiration, therefore, is a term that covers a variety of charisms, the common characteristic of which is the efficacious divine assistance to express in its purity the faith of the people of God in their formative period, in such a way as to serve as a norm for the Church in later ages.

Since inspiration is a charism freely given by God, there is no assurance that the Church, if it lost the Bible, would be able to write new scriptures that would serve the same purpose. On the contrary, there is every reason to believe that biblical inspiration is by nature confined to the formative period of the people of God, and that however perfectly modern writers succeed in expressing the faith of the contemporary Church, they cannot write scripture, which is by nature restricted to the period when the revelation was still being freshly communicated.

Recognizing its incapacity to produce new scriptures, the Church receives with great reverence and gratitude those that have been given. As we shall see, the Church makes no claim to be able to construct the true faith from its own consciousness. As a historical community it depends continually on its own origins and submits to God's word in scripture as an inviolable norm. (cf. *Dei Verbum*, no. 21)

The Church did (not) draw up the biblical canon

In opposition to Protestant claims that the Bible attests to its own inspiration, Catholic apologetic writing since the Reformation repeatedly insists that Christians would not even have a Bible were it not for the authoritative decision of the Church whereby this particular collection of ancient Jewish and Christian writings was accepted as canonical. Nowhere in the scriptures themselves does one find any statement of what books ought to be included in, or excluded from, the Church's canon. The formation of the canon was a long and complex process that took place in the course of several centuries. For its Old Testament the Church took over the sacred books which the Jews of the time regarded as scripture. As for the New Testament, various apostolic writings were read in the early Church, but one can hardly speak of anything like a canon until about the fourth century. [6]

The criteria used in drawing up the New Testament canon

were never clear and explicit, but factors such as the following
five seem to have played a major role: [7]

1. authorship by an apostle or close companion of an apostle;
2. long-standing usage in the Church;
3. in a few cases, episcopal and synodal decisions;
4. sound doctrine (as known from tradition and other recognized scriptures)
5. suitability for liturgical reading.

Interestingly enough, inspiration was not used as a criterion
of canonicity. As Everett Kalin has recently emphasized, the
early Christians looked on all authentic literature expressing the
Church's faith as divinely inspired. They excluded from the
canon many writings whose inspiration they accepted. [8] For this
reason it is correct to say that the Church by its own authoritative action constituted the collection of books we know as
scripture.

There is a danger, however, that by overemphasizing the
initiative of the Church one might end up undermining the
authority of the scriptures. If the Church had made a purely
arbitrary choice among a multitude of books, any one of which
could have been accepted as well as any other, the Church's
decision would not deserve respect. That decision has authority
if and only if it was responsible and proper. The long debates
during the early centuries among the theologians of the East and
West show that Christians attached great importance to the
decision. In deciding on the canon, the Church did not claim to
be exercising sheer administrative power, but rather to be
submitting to God's will for his Church. It is possible therefore
to say with many modern theologians, both Protestant (Barth,
Cullmann) and Catholic (Rahner, Tavard), that the scriptures
manifested themselves to the Church. The decision concerning
the canon was a submission to the authority intrinsic to the
books themselves, which by their quality demanded to be recognized as scripture. Here again, as in the case of authorship, we
encounter a mutual priority. The Church forms the Bible, but
only because the Bible, concurrently, forms the Church.
Nourished by the reading of the books from which it drew its

faith, the Church was able to discern those books which had truly nourished it, and thus to canonize them as abiding sources and norms of its own faith and worship.

The decision concerning the canon was not a simple application of external norms. Rather it was an act of discernment, which presupposed in the Church a certain affinity or connaturality with the faith to which the books bore witness. The decision concerning the canon was, in a certain sense, a charismatic one: the Church, by the power of God's Spirit, was able to recognize the books which faithfully expressed (in the formative stage) the revelation by which the Church itself still lived. [9]

The Old Testament (must/need not) be read as preparatory to the New

In connection with the two propositions just discussed, it would seem desirable to mention yet another dialectical relationship: that between the Old Testament and the New. The New Testament, as we have seen, is a direct expression of the faith of the Church, whereas the Old Testament expresses directly the faith of ancient Israel and indirectly that of the Christian Church, which finds in Israel its own prehistory.

From this it would seem that the relationship between the Old Testament and the New is simple and one-directional. The Old Testament is promise; the New is fulfillment. The Old Testament is anticipation; the New is realization. Vatican II's *Constitution on Divine Revelation* seems to authorize this view, especially by taking over from St. Augustine the dictum that the New Testament is hidden in the Old and that the Old is manifest in the New (*Dei Verbum*, no. 16). This view is by no means to be rejected. It is solidly founded in many New Testament passages. At the end of Romans, for instance, Paul declares that only through Jesus Christ can the prophetic writings be fully understood. The revelation of the mystery of God's plan of salvation which was kept secret for long ages "is now disclosed and through the prophetic writings is made known to all nations" (Rom 16:26). Again, in Corinthians, Paul declares that what was written about the Israelites in the Old Testament is intended for the instruction of us "upon whom the end of the ages has come" (1 Cor 10:11). It is in the light of Christ that we are to read and interpret what has been written in the Old Testament.

Although I personally accept the truth of what has just been said, I would add a word of caution against a simplistic understanding, which would unduly depreciate the Old Testament. It would be wrong to imagine that the Old Testament has a merely provisional value, and that everything in the Old Testament is better, more clearly, and more completely stated in the New. If that were the case, the Church could altogether dispense with the Old Testament, but of course it cannot. The *Constitution on Divine Revelation* affirms the abiding value of the Old Testament, and quite rightly, for on many points it remains unsurpassed, for example, in the sublime instructions of the prophets about God and in the models of human prayer afforded by the Psalms (cf. *Dei Verbum*, no. 15). As article 16 of the *Constitution on Revelation* points out, the two Testaments shed light upon each other. In Christian eyes the Old Testament, no doubt, needs completion by the New, but the New Testament cannot be correctly interpreted except in the light of the Old. We cannot rightly understand Jesus unless we meditate on Old Testament categories such as Son of Man and Son of God, nor can we rightly understand the God of Jesus Christ unless we recognize him as the God of Abraham, Isaac, and Jacob. Many things which lie hidden in the New Testament become evident only when we ponder the Hebrew Bible.[10]

The negative formulation of my third proposition, therefore, is necessary to prevent the Old Testament from being read as merely preparatory revelation. Catholic theology, with its characteristic ecclesiocentrism, is in danger of neglecting the Hebrew scriptures, as may be seen from the assertion of Karl Rahner that "God effected the production of the Old Testament books to the extent that they were to have a certain function and authority in the New Testament."[11] Protestant theology, with its Christo-centrism, is subject to the same tendency, especially where an exaggerated contrast is made between Law and Gospel. Some modern Lutheran theologians, from Schleiermacher to Bultmann, have tended to disparage the Jewish scriptures as documents of non-Christian religion with which Christianity ought not to be entangled.

To be rightly understood the Bible (must/need not) be read within the Church

As already stated, both the Old and New Testaments were composed to meet the religious needs of the people of God. The New Testament, in particular, was composed by churchmen seeking to respond to the liturgical, pastoral, and evangelistic concerns of the infant Church. In its decision concerning the canon, moreover, the Church selected the books which were especially suited to serve as a norm for the faith and worship of the Church in subsequent centuries. As a book drawn up for the Church's use, the Bible is quite evidently intended to be read in the Church. The ongoing life of the people of God provides the context in which the Bible can serve the purposes for which it was originally designed.

The idea that the Bible cannot be rightly used by those who do not belong to the Church has been common in controversial literature since the third century, when Tertullian wrote his famous *Prescription of Heretics.* The Bible, Tertullian insisted, belongs to the Church alone, and hence cannot be employed by heretics to mount their arguments against the Church. In our own day, it is often necessary to insist on the ecclesial character of the Bible against those religious individualists who imagine that the Bible alone, "without note or comment," ought to be able to give them all the guidance they need for their beliefs and for the conduct of their lives. In the name of faith, many have fallen into fanciful exegesis and superstitious practices. If the Bible is seen as simply one of the means by which the Church carries on its ministry and mission one need not expect the Bible to supply for every spiritual need, as certain sectarian Christians have done. But the Bible will be deeply appreciated. The Catholic Christian is convinced that God speaks through the Bible when the Bible is read in the Church, and especially in the context of the sacramental liturgy. For this reason Vatican II's

Constitution on the Liturgy asserts: "Christ is present in his word since it is he himself who speaks when the Holy Scriptures are read in the Church" (no. 7).

Although the ecclesial setting provides the normal and optimum situation for the reading of scripture, we must be on guard against domesticating the word of God or subjecting it to any kind of ecclesiastical monopoly. Vatican II in its *Decree on Ecumenism* (no. 21) quotes with approval the statement of Paul, "It [the gospel] is the power of God for salvation to everyone who has faith, to the Jew first and also to the Greek" (Rom 1:16). In the *Decree on Ecumenism*, this evidently means that Christians who are not members of the Roman Catholic Church can read the scriptures with spiritual profit. In the next sentence after this quotation, the *Decree* speaks of Protestant Christians as prayerfully reading the scriptures under the invocation of the Holy Spirit. The text in the form approved by the Council Fathers would have read: "At the prompting of the Holy Spirit, they find in the Holy Scriptures God, who speaks to them in Christ." Yet on the day before the final ceremonial vote on the entire Decree a change was introduced, as a result of an intervention of Paul VI, so that the text now reads: "Calling upon the Holy Spirit, they seek in these sacred scriptures God as he speaks to them in Christ." Certainly, there is no implication here that they seek in vain. The whole context demands that Protestants be seen as having a salvific faith in Christ, mediated by the Bible.

From experience it seems evident that the Bible has had a mighty spiritual impact upon many who live outside any Christian Church and even upon some who do not consider themselves Christians. Mahatma Gandhi, for instance, had the highest praise for the teaching of the Gospels and reproached Christians for not living up to their own religious ideals as set forth in the Sermon on the Mount. The actor Alec McCowen, who has recently stirred audiences in Britain and the United States by his rendition of the Gospel of Mark, is quoted as saying that while he does not regard himself as a Christian, he has been influenced by the Gospel he proclaims. "You can't go through it so many times," he asserts, "without some of it rubbing off." [12]

It would be too little, therefore, to regard the Bible as an instrument in the hands of the Church to be used only for the edification of its own members. God himself speaks through his word, and his voice can resound far beyond the limits of the visible Church. The *Constitution on Divine Revelation* recognizes this, especially in its last two paragraphs, where it calls for editions of the Bible for the use of non-Christians, in order that the word of the Lord may "run and be glorified" (*Dei Verbum*, no. 24-25; cf. 2 Thes 3:1). The word of God, proclaimed in the scriptures, has a power and efficacy that exceeds all human calculation. Coming from the Lord, it does not return to him empty (Is 55:10-11). [13] For this reason we do not dare to say, without qualification, that the Bible cannot be rightly understood when read outside the Church.

The Bible (must/need not) be read in a spirit of faith and prayer

The present proposition in its affirmative form demands both more and less than the preceding one. It demands more, because we cannot take it for granted that everyone who reads in the Church does so with faith and prayer. It demands less, because we cannot rule out the existence of faith and prayer among readers who are not members of the Church.

It is a commonplace that the Bible must be read in the same spirit in which it was written. This dictum, familiar to many from the *Imitation of Christ*, reappears in Benedict XV's encyclical on biblical studies and in Vatican II's *Constitution on Divine Revelation* (no. 12). From this it follows that the Bible, as an expression of faith, must be read in a spirit of faith and that since the Bible expresses devotion to the God of the Covenant, it must be read with similar devotion. Otherwise the reader, not being attuned to the biblical themes, will inevitably fail to grasp what is being said.

Or so it would seem. Before we speak too confidently we must hear both sides of the question. There is a sense in which it must be possible to read the Bible without faith. To some extent, as we have seen, the Bible is proclamation. As such it speaks to those who do not yet have Christian faith. If one could not understand it without already having faith, the Bible would be meaningless to those who most need to hear its message.

To understand what a person is saying is not the same as to believe it. Otherwise one could never disagree with another's statements. To accept or reject the claims of biblical revelation, one must first understand what those claims are. This understanding, therefore, cannot itself presuppose faith.

High-level biblical scholarship and interpretation are often done in universities and academic centers where no appeal is made to faith. The historical-critical method, which has contributed immensely to our modern understanding of the Bible, refuses to be bound by theological canons.

As scientific exegetes often point out, faith can at times interfere with an understanding of the Bible. The convinced Christian tends to imagine that the contents of Christian faith must be affirmed, or at any rate not contradicted, by the Bible, but exegetical scholarship maintains just the contrary. Raymond E. Brown, S.S., deplores the tendency of modern Catholics to read their own faith into the biblical writings. Scripture studies, he maintains, should honestly face the variety of beliefs attested in the biblical writings and help us to see the immense developments in the successive stages of revelation history. Critical scholarship in our day must not be "suffocated by pietism and exaggerated traditionalism," as has happened more than once in the past. [14]

Shall we then reverse the usual dictum and say that the Bible must be read without faith, or at least without allowing faith to influence the interpretation? I personally believe that the commitment of Christian faith is a great help insofar as it provides a foundation for understanding the matter in question. It sets up what Rudolf Bultmann called an antecedent "life-relation" to the subject matter treated in the text. [15] For the comprehension of scripture one must have at least an orientation to God and to the salvation which God makes possible. The richer sense of God provided by immersion in the Christian tradition, far from obscuring the differences between the ideas of various biblical authors and the faith of the Church today, gives an even greater sensitivity to such differences. Precisely because we have definite convictions about the God revealed in Jesus Christ, we shall find certain biblical statements surprising, even shocking. If we are unwilling to recognize and admit the differences between what we read and what we expected to find, the fault may not be that we have too much faith, but rather that we have too little. An exegete such as Raymond Brown can frankly face the problems because his faith makes him confident that the difficulties are not insoluble.

The contribution of faith and prayer varies according to the kind of biblical interpretation one is doing. When one is working on a particular phrase or sentence, and attempting to reconstruct what it would have meant to the original author and his readers, technical skills are crucially important, and religious commitments almost irrelevant. But when one is trying to grasp what the Bible as a whole has to say to the disciple in search of the path to salvation, a judicious interpretation depends on a sense of faith that can only be gained from Christian experience. For this existential kind of interpretation, faith and prayer are indispensable. The *Constitution on Divine Revelation* therefore exhorts the faithful: "Let them remember that prayer should accompany the reading of sacred Scripture, so that God and man may talk together; for we speak to him when we pray; we hear him when we read the divine sayings (Ambrose)" (*Dei Verbum*, no. 25).

The Bible alone is (not) the final criterion of Christian belief

In contrast to Protestants, who tend to look upon Christian revelation from scripture as the sole authoritative source, Catholics are accustomed to say that the Church finds the word of God in scripture and tradition. But these two sources or channels are not identical in structure. They are not two distinct quarries, each containing only a portion of the revelation. In its *Constitution on Divine Revelation* Vatican II states on two occasions (nos. 9 and 24) that scripture is the word of God, whereas of tradition it says only that it preserves and hands on the word of God (no. 9). [16] Hence it would seem that God's word, though it comes to us through tradition as well as through scripture, is not in these two sources in the same way.

This interpretation of Vatican II would harmonize with what many Catholic theologians now regard as the chief function of scripture. The Church, they hold, is a historical community, permanently dependent upon its own origins. In order to make progress, the Church must conserve the memory of its own origins and keep them in view; otherwise it could develop in a distorted manner and lose sight of its pure beginnings. In equipping the Church with inspired scriptures from the foundational period, God made it possible for the Church to keep in permanent contact with its own initial faith, and hence with God's revelation to Israel which came to completion in Jesus Christ.

From this point of view one may affirm our sixth proposition. As Karl Rahner and others have insisted, there is a Catholic *sola scriptura*. [17] Scripture is the only normative objectification of the faith of the foundational period to which we have certifiable access. If there was apostolic revelation not consigned to writing in the Bible, we have no way of identifying today what was contained in that revelation; for it has become simply inaccessible to us.

What then of the second Catholic source, sacred tradition? Christian tradition may be defined as the process of handing down the apostolic faith. In a certain sense, tradition was prior to scripture, which is a written sedimentation of it. Since the Bible was written, tradition continues to exist as the vital atmosphere in which the Bible is preached, read, and lived. Scripture does not exist alone, unaccompanied by tradition. Hence we may also assert the negative form of our sixth proposition: scripture does not function as a norm unless it is taken up into the life of the community of faith. *Scriptura nunquam sola.*

No Christian today can get at the scripture in its naked purity, unfiltered through tradition. As Paul Tillich saw very clearly, the only alternative to good tradition is bad tradition; the only alternative to a consciously held tradition is one unconsciously held. [18] The biblicist sects are not without tradition. They have very definite traditions of exegesis, dogma, and ecclesiastical style. Thus in one sense the Bible alone cannot be the final criterion. The Bible does not exist alone for any Christian today.

Still we can recognize that in the Bible-tradition couplet the two partners, though inseparable, are dissimilar. The Bible is a reliable, approved, canonical expression of the word of God; it not only transmits, but in some sense is, the word of God. Tradition does not have the same objective unassailability, for we do not possess it except under the form of a multiplicity of traditions. The many traditions of the Church have to be measured against the original deposit, as given in scripture, as a touchstone of authenticity.

This does not mean, as some biblicists contend, that the Church must remain fixed at the biblical stage of reflection and development. If the Church had remained at the primitive stage, it would not even possess canonical scriptures; for as we have seen, the Church did not seek to define its canon until about the fourth century. It is legitimate and necessary for ecclesiastical institutions, forms of worship, and formulations of the faith to develop in proportion to the needs and possibilities of later times.

The problem for the Church as it develops is to make sure that the faith is not being corrupted, that it is not being overlaid with human speculations. To sift authentic from inauthentic developments we shall have to go back repeatedly to the scriptures, which give us the pure sources of all that was later to flow forth. But we shall not be stuck with the mere letter of scripture. With the help provided by a living context of communal faith, we shall be able to make contact with the realities to which the words refer. Thanks to an experience of ,these realities in our ecclesial life of faith, we shall be capable of discerning developments that are biblically authorized, even though not logically implicit in any propositions contained in the Bible.

With the help of principles such as these it may be possible to see both the legitimacy and the culturally conditioned character of certain institutional and dogmatic developments that have occurred in the Catholic Church or in other Christian traditions. We shall not easily set aside convictions that have arisen from many centuries of devout meditation on the word of God.

In particular, we shall not subject to the caprice of the lonely Bible reader doctrines which have been authenticated by a long and stable tradition and confirmed by the decisions of the highest church authorities.

The meaning of the Bible is (not) what the human authors intended by their words

This seventh proposition is intended simply to call attention to the hermeneutical problem. There is no agreement among competent experts as to what is meant by the meaning of the Bible — let alone how that meaning is found.

Raymond E. Brown holds that the basic meaning of scripture is the literal sense, defined as "the sense which the human author directly intended and which his words convey." [19] In his recent work he holds that the real meaning of the text goes beyond the literal sense and that this larger meaning can usefully be approached through the categories of *sensus plenior* (the fuller meaning of the words) and *sensus typicus* (the meaning of the realities and events set forth in scripture).

The *Constitution on Divine Revelation*, in its cautiously worded article 12, seems to endorse two levels of meaning in the Bible. First there is the meaning intended and expressed by the human author — a meaning critically established by technical or scientific exegesis, which studies the languages, the history, and the literary forms. On a second level the Council recognizes a meaning intended by God above and beyond what could have been consciously intended by the human author. This is a theological or dogmatic meaning, to be sought out with the help of theological principles such as the following three: the unity of scripture as a whole, the exegetical tradition of the Church, and the "analogy of faith" (i.e., the coherence of the whole body of revelation as believed and taught by the Church). The Council deliberately leaves unsettled the relationship between this second level of meaning and the senses which theologians have described as fuller, typical, and spiritual. It would be scarcely consonant with Vatican II, however, to hold that there is no meaning of scripture other than that consciously intended by the human authors of the particular books. [20]

In the final chapter of the *Constitution on Divine Revelation* the use of scripture in the life of the Church is discussed. Here the Council recommends prayerful meditation on the Bible with a view to nourishing the spiritual life of the faithful. "For in the sacred books, the Father who is in heaven meets his children with great love and speaks with them; and the force and power in the word of God is so great that it remains the support and energy of the Church, the strength of faith for her sons, the food of the soul, the pure and perennial source of spiritual life" (no. 21). The Council here recognizes that the Bible is something more than a dead record to be dissected by critical analysis; it is a "precious instrument" by which God speaks to his people here and now. (cf. *Decree on Ecumenism*, no. 21). When the Bible is used in such a way that it brings about conversion, floods the soul with a deep realization of God's presence, or communicates a vivid sense of one's personal vocation, we cannot dismiss this as a mere illusion.

The question thus arises: Is there a spiritual or existential level of meaning in addition to the two levels discussed above? Exegetes and theologians, when they speak of the meaning of the Bible, generally have in mind either the meaning originally intended by the human author or a doctrine that results from the Church's meditation on the Bible as a whole in the context of Christian tradition. According to this approach, the personal insights given to those who prayerfully use the scripture to direct their lives, even though authentically communicated by God, would not be properly biblical meanings. Yet recent philosophical hermeneutics seems to suggest that the traditional concept of meaning is too narrow. Hans-Georg Gadamer, for instance, compares a classical text to a musical score, which is variously interpreted by various performers. The text, by itself, would then be considered as a normative possibility of a range of meanings to be actualized by different interpreters. From this perspective the meanings here and now mediated to particular readers within the community of faith deserve to be called meanings of the text. [21]

In pronouncing on biblical questions the magisterium (depends/does not depend) on exegetes

The last three of the ten propositions deal with the relationship between scripture scholars and the ecclesiastical *magisterium*. Since the early centuries the councils have been accustomed to cite biblical passages to support their doctrinal decisions. With some frequency after the middle of the nineteenth century, popes and Roman commissions (such as the Holy Office and the Pontifical Biblical Commission) have instructed Catholics on what they ought to hold about certain disputed biblical questions. Thus the question arises: how does the *magisterium* get its competence to settle questions which are controverted among exegetes?

Certain Catholics, such as the professor mentioned at the beginning of this paper, hold that the Church, having direct communication with the revealing God, knows what the Bible says without any dependence on biblical scholars. The popes and bishops, drawing upon their "charisms of office," can tell the biblical scholars what they are to find in the sources of revelation. Pius XII's encyclical *Humani Generis*, issued in 1950, insists on the duty of exegetes to explain scripture according to the mind of the Church, but gives no hint that the *magisterium* is in any way dependent on the work of exegetes.

However, Vatican II takes a more positive view of the contributions of biblical scholarship. It states that the preparatory work of exegetes, providing that they follow the hermeneutical rules we have discussed in the last proposition, helps to mature the judgment of the Church. All biblical interpretation, however, is finally subject to the *magisterium*, which is divinely commissioned to guard and interpret the word of God (*Dei Verbum*, no. 12). Can we infer from this that the *magisterium* is dependent upon biblical scholarship?

Ordinarily, as we shall see, the *magisterium* avoids positively imposing some one interpretation of a disputed biblical passage. It contents itself with stating the faith of the Church, which results from a meditation on all the relevant biblical passages, taken in the context of the Church's living tradition. But even for this kind of interpretation, biblical scholarship can be exceedingly useful. Biblical scholars are ordinarily consulted to ascertain the appropriateness of the biblical citations and the force of the biblical arguments used in official documents. The quality of the documents depends in part on the quality of the biblical scholarship that has gone into them. For example, the statements of the Council of Trent on the institution of the sacraments and on the grades of ordained ministry, being based on scanty biblical and historical information, suffer by comparison with the more nuanced statements of Vatican II on the same subjects.

There are of course a number of decrees from the Pontifical Biblical Commission which speak directly about disputed biblical questions. Most of these statements were issued in the first few decades of the present century, when Modernism was still seen as a threat. They reflect a generally cautious attitude with regard to new opinions — an attitude which may well have been justified at the time, in view of the inferences being drawn from novel conjecture that had not yet been sufficiently checked out either critically or theologically. These decrees may generally be defended as pastorally prudent directives for their times. From a scholarly point of view, many of these decrees are now superseded, as officials of the Biblical Commission have themselves recognized. [22]

With regard to our proposition, therefore, we may conclude that for church officials to speak persuasively and correctly about how the Bible is to be understood, they must have first listened and learned what the Bible has to say. For the *magisterium* is not above, but under, the word of God (*Dei Verbum*, no. 12). If questions arise as to how a particular text is to be interpreted according to its "literal" meaning (as defined above), the *magisterium* cannot afford to disregard technical exegesis. When the *magisterium* is speaking in general terms about matters of Christian faith, without committing itself concerning the "literal" meaning of particular texts, there will be no direct or necessary dependence on technical exegesis for the validity of the pronouncement. Even where biblical scholarship has been insufficient or faulty, the pronouncement itself may be substantially true. For it may truly express what the Church, guided by its tradition, finds in the sources of revelation taken as a whole, in light of its own lived relationship with the realities attested by scripture, including the reality of the Lord Jesus and his Holy Spirit.

The authentic interpretation of the Bible comes (not) from the magisterium alone

The affirmative form of this proposition seems to be demanded by the *Constitution on Divine Revelation*, which states: "The task of authentically interpreting the word of God, whether written or handed on, has been entrusted exclusively to the living *magisterium* of the Church, whose authority is exercised in the name of Jesus Christ" (no. 10).

Yet there is a difficulty in the translation. The word "authentic" in English commonly means "genuine," "pure," or "reliable." According to Webster's *New Collegiate Dictionary* the term "implies accordance with fact and actuality, thereby implying full trustworthiness (as, an *authentic* record)." Thus the conciliar text in English translation gives the impression that no interpretation coming from private exegetes or theologians can be genuine or trustworthy, and that interpretations given by the official teaching office of the Church are by that fact alone accurate and trustworthy.

The Latin word *authenticus*, at least in ecclesiastical usage, has a more juridical meaning. This may be illustrated from the Council of Trent, which in 1546 decreed that the Vulgate was to be considered the only authentic edition of scripture (DS, 1506).[23] In 1943 Pius XII, encouraging recourse to the original languages, was obliged to point out that Trent's decree had reference only to the *juridical* authenticity of the Vulgate and therefore did not "in any way diminish the authority and value (*auctoritatem et vim*) of the original texts."[24]

Applying a similar distinction to the matter here under discussion, we may conclude that well-founded opinions of exegetes and theologians may embody true interpretations of scripture, and, depending on the known talents of the interpreters, may enjoy a certain authority (*auctoritatem*). In that sense they may be "authentic." [25] But they do not enjoy the status of being official Church teachings—a status that belongs only to pronouncements that issue from the ecclesiastical *magisterium*. such pronouncements alone deserve to be called "authentic" in the Latin meaning of the term.

When the Church has authoritatively interpreted a text, Catholics are (not) free to interpret it otherwise.

The Council of Trent, followed by Vatican I, asserted that "holy mother Church" is mandated to judge about the true meaning and interpretation of Holy Scripture and that no one may interpret the scripture in a sense contrary to that of the Church or the unanimous consent of the Fathers (DS, 1507, 3007). Vatican II, as we have seen, teaches that the interpretation of scripture "is subject finally to the judgment of the Church, which carries out the divine commission and ministry of guarding and interpreting the word of God" (*Dei Verbum*, no. 12). The term *Church* in these texts evidently refers to the official teaching body, i.e., the *magisterium*.

These statements, however, are purely formal. In order to determine their actual force it is necessary to consider cases in which the *magisterium* has authoritatively spoken on exegetical matters.

There are several instances in which the Biblical Commission published *responsa* stating how Catholics are to interpret certain texts, such as Ps 16:10f, Mt 16:26, and Lk 9:25 (cf. DS, 3750-3751). But these *responsa*, while they may very well be true, are hardly considered authoritative today. More commonly they are regarded as statements issued to meet a past crisis in the light of the information then available, so that the texts in question would be open for reconsideration today.

It would be important for our purposes to determine whether the *magisterium* has ever used its infallible teaching power to settle definitively the meaning of any biblical text. Older editions of Denzinger's *Enchiridion* (prior to Vatican II) used to list about ten instances (if my count is correct) where the Church had allegedly defined the meaning of the text. But the more recent editions of Denzinger no longer attempt to decide which texts have actually been defined by the *magisterium*. When one puts this question to any document issued before the infallibility definition of 1870, one runs up against the difficulty that no precise distinction had yet been made between infallible definitions and other authoritative teaching. Furthermore, even at Vatican I the Fathers did not clearly indicate whether they were defining the meaning of the texts they cited in their doctrinal definitions, and, if so, whether they were defining what the text meant according to its literal sense. Thus Raymond Brown can correctly observe, with regard to the Petrine texts cited in Vatican I's definitions concerning the papacy that "experts in dogmatic theology... are not in agreement whether even in these instances the Church was defining the literal sense of scripture." [26]

With regard to the interpretation of Genesis, chapter 3, verse 15, and Revelation, chapter 12, in the bulls defining the Immaculate Conception and the Assumption, Pius IX and Pius XII did not make it clear that they intended to define the meaning, let alone the literal meaning, of the texts. Raymond Brown notes that according to many scholars the citations "imply no more than that reflection on these scriptural verses aided theologians in understanding the Marian doctrines and thus guided the Church to take a dogmatic position."[27]

Our tenth proposition raises the question whether Catholics, including exegetes and theologians, are free to interpret such texts in a sense other than that set forth in the official teaching. Allowing for the possibility of conscientious dissent under certain conditions (a question too complicated to be treated here) and for the obsolete character of certain older decrees drawn up to meet transitory crises, one may say in general terms that Catholics are not free to interpret any text in a sense repudiated by the *magisterium*. Thus, for example, if one were to hold that the reference to water "unless one is born of water and the Spirit" (Jn 3:5) is nothing but a metaphor, one would be directly contradicting the explicit teaching of Trent (DS, 1615). So, too, if one denied that the statement, "If you forgive the sins of any, they are forgiven" (Jn 20:23) referred in any genuine sense to the sacrament of penance, one would be contradicting the explicit teaching of other Tridentine canons (DS, 1703, 1710).

These exegetical pronouncements, however, are minimally restrictive. They leave the Catholic free to find many other meanings in the texts in question. To be "born of water and the Holy Spirit," even in the Johannine text, may have a much wider meaning than sacramental baptism. So too, the power to forgive sins need not be understood in the Fourth Gospel as referring *only* to sacramental absolution. Thus the Catholic is not obliged to adhere rigidly to the officially approved interpretation of these biblical texts, as though no other sense could be legitimate. There is nothing to exclude the possibility that there might be more than a single biblical meaning, or that the one meaning may not have been exhaustively stated in the official declaration, or finally, that the Holy Spirit, addressing a contemporary believer through the text, might inspire valid insights that go beyond the properly exegetical meaning of the text.

Conclusion

Since the whole purpose of this paper has been to question the validity of simple, undialectical statements, it is scarcely possible to draw any unequivocal conclusion. In addressing each of our ten issues we have seen that neither a simple affirmation nor a simple negation is adequate, though both the affirmative and negative form of our propositions may be defended. In discussing such matters one must become accustomed to think and speak dialectically. We are at every point dealing with mutual priorities, reciprocal dependence, and coinherence. Just as it is true to say that the Church forms the sacraments while the sacraments form the Church, so, too, we may say, the Church creates the Bible while the Bible creates the Church. The Bible authenticates tradition, but tradition authenticates the Bible. The *magisterium* learns from biblical scholars and at the same time instructs them what they are to believe about scripture.

The Bible is the Church's book, but the Church is under the Bible as the word of God. The Bible is not the Church, but the Church can never be without the Bible, nor can the Bible be truly Bible without the Church. Between Bible and Church there is both a profound unity and an ineradicable distinction.

As suggested in our opening paragraphs, the questions dealt with in this paper have not only an intra-Catholic but an ecumenical importance. It may therefore be fitting to give the last word to a distinguished ecumenist, George Tavard. In a frequently quoted paragraph he eloquently expresses the unity-in-difference between Bible and Church:

> The secret of re-integration, or of Christian unity, or of a theology of ecumenism (whatever name we choose to give this) may lie in opening a way back to an inclusive concept of scripture and of the Church. Scripture cannot be the word of God once it has been severed from the Church which is the Bride and the Body of Christ. And the Church could not be the Bride and the Body, had she not received the gift of understanding the word. These two phases of God's visitation of man are aspects of one mystery. They are ultimately one, though one in two. The Church implies the scripture as the scripture implies the Church. [28]

INSPIRATION AND THE ORIGINS OF THE NEW TESTAMENT

William S. Kurz, S.J.

Introduction

Both the Church at large and the charismatic renewal are still gradually discovering the wide-ranging implications of the Vatican II *Dogmatic Constitution on Divine Revelation* for interpreting scripture. George Martin's *Reading Scripture as the Word of God* is a masterful introduction to the Vatican II approach, written for the layperson.[1] From my own use of this book in university undergraduate courses and in Bible teachings to laypeople, I find it helpful for showing Christians — ranging from traditional Catholics to those with *sola scriptura* and fundamentalist backgrounds — the reasonableness of the Vatican II perspective on scripture.

However, the full implications of the belief that the scriptures are both fully divine and fully human need to be still further explicated in the light of the New Testament evidence. Only in this way do I see a way to break out of some current impasses in the renewal regarding scriptural interpretation, which have such practical consequences as reluctance to give leadership roles to women because of an ahistorical reading of 1 Tm 2:8-15. The consequences of the Council's teaching on *Sacred Scripture, Its Inspiration and Divine Interpretation*, and on the human conditioning of New Testament passages, including the limitations intrinsic to this humanness, seem to preclude an absolutized view of the authority for the twentieth-century Church of such New Testament passages taken alone. Not only does the Council continue to insist on the need to consult Church tradition and authority in interpreting scripture, but the implications of the human language of scripture itself have not been fully realized. Just as many Christians still cannot fully appreciate the "scandal" of God's "condescension" in sending his divine Son in fully human form, so do they have a similarly strong "docetic" tendency in dealing with scripture as the word of God "expressed in human language."[2]

The purpose of this paper is to flesh out, with evidence from the New Testament itself, more of the implications of the Council teaching which states that scripture is the inspired word of God in fully human words of men, with all the historical, cultural, and even cognitive limits this *necessarily* implies. This does not arise from an apriori desire to explain away difficult texts of the Bible, a tendency I vigorously oppose and lament. Nor does it stem from the desire to import into biblical religion twentieth-century conceptions that in fact have no place therein. It is rather the result of years of trying to do the exegetical work asked of scholars by the Council, and the strong realization that the facts in the biblical texts themselves belie some of the uses of scripture and interpretations of inspiration which I have encountered during ten years' experience in the charismatic renewal. On the other hand, this reconstruction of the origins of the Church and of the New Testament in the light of the New Testament evidence is an equally strong rejoinder to the reductionism of much current scholarship, which fails to give sufficient weight to the reality of the miraculous, to the divinity of Jesus, and to scripture as the inspired word of God.

Three convictions lie behind this attempt to use the New Testament evidence of the humanity of these writings to deepen our understanding of inspiration. (1) The way inspiration is understood heavily influences how scripture is interpreted.[3] (2) Vatican II stressed further the human dimensions of the scriptures and rejected a psychological picture of inspiration that would have God dictating or putting the very thoughts and words into the minds of the writers, who simply recorded them (as does a modern secretary). (3) The evidence from the texts themselves about how they were written and gathered into our New Testament is very important for understanding what God's inspiration means and thus for knowing how to read and interpret the New Testament as God's word written in the words of men.

As Alois Grillmeier wrote in his careful commentary on the chapter of *On Revelation* that deals with inspiration and interpretation, the document tries to purify the Church from mechanistic ways of understanding how God inspires human authors, and instead to point to ways that leave more room for the personalities of the human authors.[4] The document does not call God the literary author (*auctor litterarius*) in the literal sense; this term is reserved for the human authors. Yet God has a true influence on the writers. The Council gives no detailed explanation of how this takes place and refrains from teaching that the authors were aware of this inspiration. It puts a much stronger emphasis than previous Church teaching did on the human share in creating the sacred books. The study of earlier rejected drafts of this document on revelation indicates conscious rejection of such previously common terms for the human authors as "living instruments." Also avoided is the familiar expression that God is the "principal author" (*auctor principalis*). Rather, the writers are called "true authors," and their own differences and limitations are expressed in the recognition of the "use of their own powers and abilities" (*On Revelation*, Art. 11). "In spite of this God achieves his aim with them."[5] The Council leaves it to theologians to explain, on the basis of the history of the text, how God and man cooperate.

Clues from Scriptural Authors about Inspiration

What are some insights into the meaning of inspiration which we can glean from statements of the New Testament writers themselves? In the first place, we find that there exists among the writers a spectrum of explicit awareness of God's inspiration, or at least of the acknowledgment of that inspiration. John, the prophet and author of Revelation, explicitly calls his writing a revelation and a prophecy (Rv 1, 22, passim), and like other prophets and apocalyptic writers, he relates the command that he was given to write what he sees and hears. Such heightened awareness of inspiration is common to the Old Testament prophetic books, and goes beyond the ordinary inspiration of most of the books of Old and New Testaments in mentioning explicit revelation experienced by the writer as such. This pattern seems to be linked to the peculiar nature of the prophets' experience, not to biblical authorship as such. Such prophetic experience seems analogous to contemporary prophecy in the renewal.

At the more "secular" end of the spectrum, where there is no acknowledgment that the writer is inspired, is the prologue to Luke-Acts: There the author, who often refers to the Spirit guiding Jesus or Christian missionaries in what they do and say, makes no mention of the Spirit or of inspiration or divine guidance and describes his own procedure as author in technical secular language. He simply says "It seemed good to me also . . . to write for you, most excellent Theophilus, so that you may know the certainty of the things which you have been taught" (Lk 1:3-4). He also mentions his sources, his predecessors in writing "an account" (a neutral term compared to Mark's "Gospel"), and the research and work he did for his own account. Even granting the fact that he is using a secular form of prologue and dedication, it still seems significant that he shows no realization that his account was inspired by God. One gets the same impression from the prologue of 2 Mc 2:19-32, which goes into considerable detail about the author's work in digesting Jason of Cyrene's five books into one, and his desire to please his readers, without the slightest hint that he realized he was inspired to do this by the Holy Spirit. Nor does the author of Colossians seem to be aware of any difference in authority or inspiration between the two letters he was writing to the two churches of Colossae and Laodicea, which he asks the churches to exchange between them (Col 4:16). Of these two letters, only that to the Colossians is part of our New Testament and therefore accepted by the Church today as inspired. The other is lost.

In his letters Paul shows no awareness of any inspiration by God to write other than his consciousness of the need to exercise his apostolic authority and responsibility for the congregation addressed. By contrast, he does say that he was told in a revelation to go to Jerusalem (Gal 2:1-2). A later letter, 2 Peter, talks of Paul's letters as a group (at least some were collected by that time), and treats them in the same category as the Old Testament: "The ignorant...distort them (just as they do the rest of scripture) to their own ruin" (2 Pt 3:16). But Paul himself never talks of his own letters as in the same category with scripture, which is his main authority. He does insist that he has the Spirit of God (1 Cor 7:40), and even shares mysteries that he knows (1 Cor 15:51, Rom 11:25ff). In the latter passage, his expectation that all his fellow Jews would be converted causes a problem because it does not seem likely to come true, despite Paul's sense of revelation. These observations suggest that the inspiration of scriptural writings is not to be sought primarily in the writer's experience of such inspiration or of revelation by God, nor does such experience seem inseparably linked to the accuracy of the resulting statement. In Paul's case, the experience of God's guidance appears more closely related to his role as an apostle with prophetic gifts, than to his role as a writer of an inspired book.

All such evidence suggests that perhaps God's inspiration of these writers took the form of his influence on their lives and his providential guidance, without necessarily any concomitant awareness on the part of the writers that they were being especially inspired or guided to write. This confirms the value of empirical study of the New Testament evidence to determine how the books did come to be written. Since Vatican II, Catholics have also become more aware of how closely interrelated the origins of the New Testament are with the origins of the Church itself. Somehow, the process of God's guidance and inspiration includes not just the writing of the final drafts of the Old and New Testament documents but the witness, life, oral traditions, and teaching of the people of God itself, both Israel in the Old Testament and the Church in the New Testament.

Theories of the Origins of the Church and the New Testament

Most of the scholarly reconstructions of the origins of the Church use a linear model of evolution. In 1912, Wilhelm Heitmüller proposed the predominant hypothesis that traced this evolution from Jesus to "Primitive Christianity" to "Hellenistic Christianity" to Paul.[6] Influential writers who made similar proposals include Bousset, Bultmann, Conzelmann and Reginald Fuller. Most readily available in Perrin's introduction, these linear models of evolution portray the period after Paul as dominated by the traumatic fall of Jerusalem and then a final stage of decline and institutionalization called "Early Catholicism" (*Frühkatholizismus*).[7]

Behind such reconstructions lie several presuppositions and even prejudices which make them implausible and unacceptable. The one most widely recognized of late is the complex of Enlightenment presuppositions. Characterized by rationalism, this complex includes the refusal to accept the reality of miracles, visions, prophecies, revelations, or any kind of direct divine intervention, which are all seen as violations of the "natural order" of a (now passé) Newtonian universe. This rationalism is the main thrust behind Bultmann's program of demythologizing the Bible.

Less widely recognized, and therefore more necessary to develop here, are the prejudices behind most of these theories of Church origins. Stemming mostly from German Evangelical scholars in the first half of this century, these reconstructions have a strong bias against both Judaism and Catholicism.[8] This bias involves a strong tendency to read the first-century texts as a clash between Law and Gospel. The "pure Gospel" is found only in Paul and John, before the later disciples of Paul "tamed" him by writing the "orthodox" Pastoral Letters, and the later "ecclesiastical redactors" reordered, added to, and "toned down" the Evangelist John. Bultmann's *Theology of the New Testament* and commentary on John are classic representatives of this bias.[9] After Paul and John, this view sees a dramatic decline from their powerful Gospel to "Early Catholicism."

This decadent form of Christianity (continued of course in the Roman Catholic Church) is seen to have resulted from three movements: legalism, magic sacramentalism, and institutionalism. First, from Jewish Christians came the tendency to reintroduce Jewish *legalism* (anti-Jewish bias as well). Second, from pagan Christians came the tendency to magic and superstition and *sacramentalism*. The anti-Catholic slant of this is evident. But there is also a note of hostility to the miraculous here, as seen especially in comparisons to Hellenistic magic and "divine men" miracle-mongering. Other biases behind such analogies include the Enlightenment rationalism mentioned above and signs of hostility to the "enthusiasm" of the Radical Reformation, which has similarities to the charismatic revival in Pentecostal and mainline churches today.

The third element of "Early Catholicism" is the decline from the freedom of the early Gospel back into *institutionalism*, which is seen as the unfortunate result of the struggle by second and third generation Christians against what they considered heretics. In fact, an extremely influential book by Walter Bauer actually glorifies and gives primacy to early Christian "Heresy" (read post-Reformation multiplicity of Christian denominations) over "Orthodoxy" (read the Roman Catholicism of a Pius IX).[10]

Though these theories of the pollution of the pure Gospel by a combination of Jewish legalism, pagan superstitious sacramentalism, and institutionalism actually are predominant in contemporary New Testament scholarship, they are so heavily influenced by these prejudices as to be extremely suspect. Such hidden presuppositions have for decades been used to interpret the data, and the result has often been a refusal to let the New Testament evidence speak on its own terms. New Testament writings are labelled, categorized, and either over-emphasized or ignored, often under the rubric of a "canon within the canon." Overwhelming evidence for the Jewish roots of most of Christianity and for the heavy use of the Old Testament by virtually all the New Testament tends to be ignored as scholars comb the Hellenistic writings for parallels. The most blatant political ramification of this was the Nazi burning of a book by a

Norwegian scholar in 1941 which clearly demonstrated these Jewish roots of Christianity.[11]

Another presupposition (shared by Bultmann) which invalidates much in these theories is the relegation of Jesus' (Jewish) earthly ministry to the level of pre-Christian presuppositions of New Testament theology. This view seems to arise out of a combination of skepticism about what can be historically known about Jesus and a deliberate lack of interest in the career of Jesus before his death and resurrection, often in the interests of the "pure Pauline Gospel" or the earliest Christian kerygma. This ignores the obvious effect that Jesus had on his disciples during the time they travelled with him. After all, he did teach and influence his disciples. In the light of the resurrection these disciples remembered what he said and did, and they imitated his style of life and ministry and teaching. The evidence suggests far more continuity between Jesus and his disciples than most of these hypotheses admit.

In place of such linear reconstructions based on the preceding presuppositions and tendencies, I would rather propose a model of a huge ripple caused by the "splash" of the Christ event and expanding outward simultaneously in all directions. The linear model can give the impression that the various kinds of Christianity succeeded each other temporally and that Christianity developed in the same way all over. This has led to dating certain documents as late, merely because they exhibit a "developed" Christology or institutional form. Rather, many of these developments were occuring at the same time in different communities. Some linear theories also make a non-viable distinction between "Palestinian" and "Hellenistic" and often imply a lack of contact between the two.

But rather than continually compare my model to previous proposals, and to avoid merely reacting to what others have written, I would prefer to propose my own reconstruction of these crucial events. Either to prove or to defend this hypothesis against all alternatives would take much more space and time than is available. Some of the concerns that this theory emphasizes more than most theories are: (1) the continuities as well as differences between Jesus and his disciples; (2) both the unity and variety of early Christianity; (3) the relationship between earliest Christianity and the later Church; (4) and comparable experiences of development in the contemporary renewal and the Church at large. It will try to avoid anti-Jewish, anti-Catholic, and anti-Pentecostal slants, as well as hypercritical skepticism about the historical Jesus and excessive dichotomizing of different kinds of Christianity seen as in mutual opposition, a tendency which seems to be reading the splits following the Protestant Reformation back into the New Testament evidence.[12]

The Beginnings

The origins of both the Church and the New Testament go back to the ministry of Jesus himself. This might seem self-evident if it were not so frequently disputed. Jesus healed. He preached to crowds, proclaiming the imminent coming of God's Kingdom. The kinds of stories we have about Jesus, his sayings in the Gospels, the way in which many sources stress his authority and miracles, and the evidence of how other persons reacted to him — all suggest some conviction on his part that the coming of the Kingdom was closely related to and even incipiently realized in his ministry. But Jesus not only preached to the crowds, he also formed a small group of close disciples who, like himself, left their homes and travelled with him as he preached throughout the country. These men would not have left their homes and livelihoods to follow a wandering preacher and healer if they had not been deeply impressed with him, even if they did not always understand him.

Such a conclusion is not a form of psychologizing. It follows directly from a principle frequently overlooked by those who claim almost complete discontinuity between Jesus and the Church, or between the "Jesus of history and the Christ of faith." The principle is that every effect requires a proportionate cause. The profound effect on the disciples is clear evidence of the impact Jesus made on them. Even before the resurrection, they left their homes to follow him. After the resurrection, they were transformed into fearless witnesses, most of whom died martyrs' deaths for Jesus. Such effects are convincing evidence of the powerful impact Jesus made, both before and after his resurrection.

The powerful influence of Jesus on his disciples is confirmed by comparable situations regarding teachers and disciples. In the master-disciple relationship among the Old Testament prophets, in the wisdom traditions, among Greek philosophers, and the later Jewish rabbis, the disciples learned both the master's teaching (even if they did not memorize it verbatim) and his way of life. Imitation of the master and handing on his teaching are common behavior for these circles.

Jesus taught and trained his disciples for the purpose of extending his ministry and message beyond the people he himself was physically able to meet. Otherwise there would have been no reason to select closer disciples from among the crowds. If only because they travelled and lived with him, Jesus was able to teach these disciples at a deeper level than the crowds in general. The core of this group of disciples consisted of men who were being trained for the same kinds of teaching and healing that Jesus performed, but women also were part of the group who wandered homeless with Jesus (Lk 23:49; 8:1-3). Their role seems primarily to have been to minister to Jesus and the men. At least there is no hint that they preached to the crowds directly (see Acts 1-2 for a similar pattern after the resurrection).

One thing most historians are now beginning to admit more than previously is that Jesus had a strong premonition of his coming violent death, not unrelated to his strongly attested clashes with religious authorities over his association with sinners, his "violation" of the Sabbath and other traditions, and his preaching of repentance in view of the imminence of the Kingdom of God. It is most historically probable that Jesus tried to warn his disciples of his death and to prepare them for it. We are fairly sure that he demanded of his disciples willingness to face death for his sake.

One occasion of preparing the disciples for his death was probably "the last supper." Hans Schürmann has argued at length for the historical probability that the sufficient cause needed to explain the Eucharist in the earliest Church is a farewell meal with Jesus in which he asked his disciples to remember him in the breaking of the bread and sharing of the cup.[13]

For the passion itself we are comparatively well-informed. Most scholars agree that the passion account is the earliest attempt to chronicle the events of Jesus' life in the order in which they happened, although Christians obviously described these events in the light of the resurrection and their meditation on the Old Testament.[14] The main lines of the account are attempts to give factual accounts of how Jesus was arrested, condemned, crucified, and buried. These facts and their interpretation were potential obstacles to the Christian message and had to be explained. The intent is heavily apologetic, but if the facts were not accurate, apologetic based on them would be worthless, if not actually counterproductive. As a result of Jesus' death, his band of disciples was scattered or in hiding.

Luke's Emmaus narrative (Lk 24), though obviously paradigmatic and symbolic of the Christian Eucharist, gives a description of the mind-set of the disciples right after Jesus' death that is a very plausible historical reconstruction: The disciples' hopes, which had centered on the man Jesus, who was now removed at the instigation of the religious leaders, had been shattered. Even the first reports of the empty tomb seemed to them delirious. Jesus' death would have destroyed his work and scattered and demoralized his disciples if it had not been followed quickly by the discovery of the empty tomb and appearances of the raised Jesus to many disciples. That is also Luke's opinion and the reason he describes the contrasting failures of other messianic movements after the death of their leaders in Acts 5:35-37. The sufficient cause needed to explain the transformation of the disciples from the fearful men who abandoned Christ at the passion to the courageous preachers who faced arrest are the various appearances of Christ, which assured them that Jesus was raised and vindicated by God, plus their experience of receiving the Spirit, which gave them courage and power to witness, preach, and heal in Jesus' name. Even unbelieving historians marvel at the astoundingly rapid spread of the Church. Believers can rightly point to the improbability of such growth if the originally weak disciples had not been religiously fortified in a striking way.

Theories of the beginning of the Church that do not so account for the specifically religious experience of the first disciples cannot satisfactorily explain what happened. James D.G. Dunn's *Jesus and the Spirit* is an attempt to reconstruct the kinds of religious experiences of the first disciples needed to explain the astounding growth of the early Church.[15] He dialogues with the scholarly literature and dissents with most of it by arguing that the undisputed primacy of the "mother church" Jerusalem (whose primacy even Paul did not contest) and the absence of any mention of a Galilean church at this time support Luke and John over against Mark and Matthew in locating the risen Christ's first appearances in Jerusalem, not in Galilee. He relates these appearances to the independent discovery by the women that the tomb was empty.

Dunn argues plausibly that some such major preaching event as the Pentecost account in Acts chapter 2 is needed to describe the sudden appearance of a large Jerusalem church, even if the account has been highly theologized in Luke's telling. For example, the resurrection appearance to 500 brethren at once, most of whom were alive in the fifties and could be questioned about it, occurred very early (it is mentioned before the appearance to James), probably in the Jerusalem church (1 Cor 15:6-7). It presupposes a very large gathering of disciples soon after Jesus' passion.

Dunn's explanation seems a far more plausible historical reconstruction of the first beginnings of the Easter Church than Marxsen's, which has heavily influenced most scholarly theories.[16] The implication of Marxsen's book, even if never directly stated, is to deny that the tomb was discovered empty and to attribute the whole resurrection tradition to a vision Peter had. This approach to the resurrection and origins of the Church seems to be the most common one among German and American scholars, who frequently treat Luke's account as mere theological fiction. It is often taught even in Catholic colleges and seminaries and has influenced Catholic religious education and publishing.[17]

The appearances of the risen Jesus and the experience of

receiving the power of his Spirit led the disciples to the conviction that the Kingdom of God that Jesus had preached was now coming and that they were living in the last days. The outpouring of the Spirit which they experienced corresponded to scriptural expectations that the Spirit would be poured out in the last days. In Acts, chapter 2, Luke links these experiences with scriptural predictions and expectations in order to provide a plausible theological explanation of evidence (found also in the early Pauline letters) that the first Christians experienced the Spirit in powerful ways; that they believed they were living in the last days predicted in scripture; and that they expected the second coming of Jesus to occur during their lifetime.

First Generation Christianity

The first Christian missionary outreach was to Jews. Though the original disciples of Jesus were Galilean Jews, at least their leaders — James, Peter, and John — made Jerusalem their headquarters (Gal 1-2). As the pilgrimage center for diaspora Jewry, Jerusalem drew Jews from around the world, and its Christians were from all the Jewish groups. Few scholars doubt that the Jerusalem community had both Jews who spoke the language of Palestine (Aramaic), as did the original disciples, and those who spoke only or primarily Greek, the international language (Acts 6). Luke tells us it was these Hellenistic Jews who were primarily responsible for the early outreach to other Hellenistic cities, preaching first to Greek-speaking Jews but eventually also to non-Jews (Acts 8-11). Already at this earliest stage there must have been a translation of some of Jesus' Aramaic sayings into Greek, the language of the New Testament.

The remarkably rapid expansion of Christianity was the result of an extraordinary missionary outreach of the first disciples to pockets of Jews both in Palestine and in major cities nearby. A few years after Jesus' death, when Paul was converted, there was already a Christian community in the Hellenistic city of Damascus outside Palestine (Gal 1:17; Acts 9). Antioch, far to the north, was itself an early center for further missionary outreach (see Gal 2; Acts 11 & 13).

Since the first preaching was to Jews, it naturally emphasized that Jesus was the Messiah of Jewish expectation and used the Jewish scripture to explain and substantiate Christian claims for Jesus. From the beginning, Christian Jews used simple confessions of faith in Jesus and a basic kerygma of Jesus' death and resurrection according to the scriptures (Rom 1:3-4). Catechesis to these Jews in the Christian way of living probably made heavy use of the sayings of Jesus, since these would be the only elements that were distinct from what they already practiced as Jews.

To convince the Jews, it was particularly important to demonstrate that Jesus was innocent and that he suffered "for our sins according to the scriptures" (1 Cor 15:3). Many scholars think that a passion account was constructed in this first Jewish phase to show this. The Eucharist commemorating Jesus' saving death seems to have existed from the beginning. It took place in the context of a community meal, presupposed the Jewish format of blessings, and imitated Jesus' table fellowship with his disciples (see 1 Cor 11). Its format may well have been influenced as well by the Passover meal and ritual, which included an explanation of the rite as signifying the people's salvation from Egypt. For the Eucharist too linked a rite to salvation in Jesus.

The kind of reading and preaching of scripture the first Christians did was probably based on the synagogue format of reading and explaining the Old Testament, combined in their worship services with praying the psalms and other prayers. Even today, liturgists make heavy use of Jewish antecedents to explain both the service of the Word and the Eucharistic meal.

A crisis of identity for the young Church arose when pagans began to be converted directly to Christianity without first becoming Jews by circumcision. Beginning in the Hellenistic city of Antioch (and possibly elsewhere at the same time), this practice would later cause the bitter Judaizing controversies Paul faced. As long as the first Christians were all Jews, both Jews and Christians saw incipient Christianity as one of several forms of Judaism, distinguished by its belief in Jesus as Messiah, but still sharing in Jewish practice and worship.

A modern analogy to this might be a Catholic parish charismatic prayer community, which shares in the parish worship but also has its own prayer meetings. If such a group, which began in a parish and is seen by themselves and other parishioners as part of the parish, began to take into itself non-Catholics who obviously could not belong to the parish, there would be confusion about its identity as part of the parish. If this were to lead to a final break with the parish and with Catholicism for a "nondenominational" charismatic parish, that would seem a close analogy with the process of earliest Christianity's involvement in Judaism, eventual inclusion of non-Jews, and final split off into a new religion. Obviously, as the modern analogy illustrates, such a final step was a traumatic one, both for the Jewish Christians and for "the old parishioners" — the non-Christian Jews who were left behind or who expelled the Christians from their synagogues. This trauma has left its mark in New Testament descriptions of Christian-Jewish hostility and has to be taken into account if contemporary Christians are not to fall into an anti-Jewish reading of the New Testament, as so often happens.

We have seen that already in earliest Christianity there was great variety in the cultural, religious, and national backgrounds of Christians. To return to our analogy of an expanding ripple from the impact of the Christ event, the incipient ripple would consist of the first generation of converts to Christianity. A ripple does not expand along isolated lines or trajectories but goes outward in several directions at once, maintaining some contact along the whole outward thrust. The New Testament evidence, supplemented by what we know of the frequency of travel along trade routes in the first century, strongly suggests that the churches in major centers were not isolated from one another but in communication. The very phenomenon of letters, the descriptions of the travels of Paul and other wandering prophets and apostles, Paul's collection from all his churches for Jerusalem, the use of Mark's Gospel in two different churches by Luke and Matthew, the many traditional materials in John as well — all point to interaction between the separate churches, even as their diversity increased. And all of them were still focused on salvation in Jesus and living his way.

As different people looked at Jesus from different perspectives and situations, a variety of theologies arose, which are reflected in the various New Testament books. As different theologies were tested in various churches and by authorities such as Paul and the writer of 1 John, some of them were found to be untrue to the Christian message and were rejected as heresy. This concern for genuine doctrine and moral practice did not just arise in the later New Testament books, but is already obvious in Paul, the earliest writer. The phenomenon of diversification of Christian responses to the same Jesus and the concern for the orthodoxy of these responses is important for how we interpret the New Testament and the differences within it. As Christians, we believe that this whole process was guided and inspired by God, who uses even human differences, error, weakness, and sin in achieving his saving plan.

In some quarters today, the notion of each person being his or her own judge in interpreting the Bible, in questions of doctrine and on moral issues, is backed by a view of the development of authority in the Church which is not supported by the sum of the New Testament evidence. Both Old and New Testament documents overwhelmingly stress the need for salvation, not as isolated individuals but as part of a people or community or church. Whenever there is a group, there must be at least informal leadership if the group is to hold together and grow. All the evidence points to the fact that, from the beginning, there were (apostolic) founders of churches, leaders, teachers, pastors, preachers, prophets, and the like, who converted, taught, corrected, guided, and at times expelled members. The earliest evidence does not show any clear pattern of names and structures for local authorities in all the various communities. But it does suggest that if founders did not stay on to lead the churches they had begun, local authorities (often subordinate to the travelling apostle who founded the group) were in charge. We have, for example, evidence from Paul that he wanted certain local people to be obeyed in his absence (e.g., see 1 Cor 16:15-18, 1 Thes 5:12-13).[18] Philippians is addressed to the Christians and their bishops and deacons. Philemon seems to be the head of one house-church. The common thesis in scholarly literature that organization and authority figures were the mark of a later decline into "Early Catholicism" from the charismatic freedom of the more utopian Pauline communities is a caricature that overlooks the evidence for the existence of authority figures from the beginning.[19]

The most important variations among the many New Testament churches for understanding the New Testament writings are the diverse mixtures of Jewish and Gentile Christians in those churches. At least since the forties, there were Christians who were converted directly from paganism without first becoming Jews. Many of these pagans had already been interested in Judaism, admired the monotheism and high morality of the Jews, and attended Jewish synagogues and learned Jewish scripture. They did not actually become Jews because they did not want circumcision and the whole Jewish Law, which would have cut them off from their relatives and business associates. Known as "Godfearers," they were particularly open to Christian preaching which did not require the whole Jewish Law. Thus, much of the early Christian missionary expansion was along trails already beaten by diaspora Jews. For these converts, even though they were not Jews, the Old Testament was an extremely important part of their Christianity.

The mixture of Jewish and Gentile Christians ranged from the predominantly Jewish-Christian communities with some Gentile members (e.g., probably Matthew's later community) to a more even mixture (probably those addressed in the letter to the Romans) to those almost totally Gentile Christian (as those addressed in 1 Thessalonians).

In most cases, the extent of syncretism with Hellenistic religions and philosophies in the congregations was directly related to the extent of the admixture of converted pagans in any one community. However, already in the Greek translation of the Old Testament and in intertestamental literature and the proselytizing and apologetics of diaspora Judaism, Jewish and Old Testament religious thought was translated into Hellenistic categories and approaches. For example, the Greek notions of an immortal soul did influence the Greek Book of Wisdom, but in a Jewish form. Hellenistic syncretism was already present in Judaism, and thus it existed among Jewish Christians as well as converted pagans.

Also, *all* Christian converts, whether from Judaism or paganism, were taught the meaning of Jesus through the Old Testament, so that the Old Testament is important for understanding all the New Testament writings, not just the more heavily Jewish ones. In the Roman world, which saw many strange and new religions, it was important to demonstrate that your religion was not a novelty but quite old. The Christians did this by appropriating the Jewish scripture for themselves. Arguments about the antiquity of the religion were very important to prospective pagan converts.[20]

Another use of the Old Testament important to prospective pagan converts was proof from prophecy. Pagan religion in the first century put great stock in oracles and their fulfillment. If one could show that an event had been predicted in an oracle, that would constitute strong proof for that religion. Among pagan Christians, this pagan view of prophecies as oracles of the future became mixed with the more biblical notion of prophecy as God's message to the immediate generation. However, even in the Bible there are several understandings concerning prophecy, including one which emphasized that it foretold the future (found in Jewish apocalyptic, which was popular from about 200 B.C. to 200 A.D.). In other words, dichotomies between Jewish and Gentile Christianity are oversimplifications and tend to be inaccurate. Thus, if one insists on making such a dichotomy, one must also recognize that proof from Old Testament prophecy was as important for Gentile Christians as for Jewish Christians. Even much later, Justin Martyr, a converted pagan who wrote from 140 to 160 A.D., considered himself a Greek philosopher when he demonstrated his philosophy from Old Testament prophecies.

Some of the ways syncretism appears in the New Testament writings is in the use of language common to religious mysteries, astrology, and various kinds of philosophic missionaries. Converted pagans would perhaps tend to put more stress on Jesus as Lord of the cult worship than Jewish Christians would.[21] Some of the Christ hymns in the New Testament seem to reflect such cultic background (e.g., Phil 2:6-11). Occasional New Testament passages (e.g., Colossians) may be opposing astrological speculation.

Similarly, many of the instructions found in the New Testament letters concerning ethical and family life and relations to the state are simply taken over from philosophical lists of virtues and vices and household duties. Though many of these are from the second generation, they can be mentioned in connection with this phenomenon of syncretism. They come more from the first-century culture *to* which the Gospel was spoken than *from* the Gospel itself. This is an important analogy for the use of twentieth-century ethical positions (such as a more adult role for women, who are now equally educated with men, versus the first century, when women in most cultures tended to be treated as *minors*, under the authority of either their father or their husband). Some of the New Testament teachings on women's roles are simply statements of what was held by the culture (reflecting inferior education and opportunities for women) and may not be immediately applicable to later and different cultures.

What were the New Testament materials in circulation during this first generation (say, until the death of Paul and Peter in the mid-sixties)? Obviously, various churches had individual letters from Paul, but they were not yet collected together, and at least some of them were lost. Of the traditions that were later incorporated into the Gospels, kerygmatic, confessional, and liturgical material was available in the churches. Many isolated sayings of Jesus and stories about his great deeds were also remembered and told, especially in moral exhortation and as examples for imitation. In fact it seems that collections of the sayings did exist. Some were connected orally by such mnemonic devices as key catch words (e.g., light of the world, light on a mountain, light under a bushel, etc.). Some were written in Greek, especially as the association with eyewitnesses lessened because of time or distance from the beginnings of Christianity. There is also evidence for collections of stories of Jesus' miracles at a pre-Gospel date (e.g., the "Signs Source" of

John). Various churches probably had different oral and written collections of sayings and stories, as well as early forms of a continuous passion narrative.

At the beginning of the second generation, in the late sixties and early seventies, the first Gospel writer (probably Mark) collected these materials, made a selection from them, and wove them into a continuous narrative about Jesus, from his baptism by John to the empty tomb. It is important to emphasize that the first Gospel writer had gathered mostly unconnected stories and sayings from various sources and would have had no way of knowing in what order the sayings or stories took place. One of his tasks was to put them into some plausible order (e.g., "write in order," Lk 1:3, is a technical term for this in Hellenistic historiography). Mark's order is followed in the main by Matthew and Luke, but both do change the order of occasional sayings and stories. John's order is usually quite different, except for the events that obviously began or ended Jesus' ministry.

Mark's Gospel seems to have been written under a situation of trauma, quite possibly a little after the persecution of Christians under Nero in Rome (during which both Peter and Paul were probably martyred) and around the time of the Jewish war which saw the destruction of Jerusalem and the temple. Crisis times breed the crisis literature known as apocalyptic, and Mark's Gospel has a decidedly apocalyptic cast to it, much more than the other three.

All the evidence and reconstruction thus far given suggests a different way of perceiving the inspiration of the New Testament books than is common. God's inspiration and guidance would seem primarily evident in his providential guidance of this whole process of the spread of Christianity, which included the gathering and writing of Jesus material and of apostolic letters by many people in many places and the gathering, ordering, and interpreting of the material about Jesus by the first Gospel writer. Human beings were acting in very human ways through all this, but we believe that God was guiding it all in his providence. Much of the guidance took place in the pre-literary phase of the missionaries' prayer and apostolic decisions, as when Paul was led in one direction rather than another

(Gal 2:2), or when he felt the need to address the problems of one of his churches. The pastoral decisions to gather, preserve, and write down the stories and sayings of Jesus, as well as the decision of the first Gospel writer that his church needed a consecutive account that would order and preserve all these isolated materials were also guided by God. But, as in the case of Luke, the writer may not have experienced this as direct psychological prompting by God. It could just as well have come from his habitual life of trying to do God's will and to serve his people, combined with the awareness that the churches needed something like this.

Another conclusion made above which affects how we interpret what God's message within a New Testament writing is for today is that the cultural and historical context contributes to the actual message and wording of a passage. The phenomenon of syncretism shows how certain teachings in the New Testament, such as some on women's roles, come more from the first-century culture *to* which the word of God is spoken than *from* God himself as timeless teaching. As in prophecy, the word of God is always spoken (or written) for concrete situations. We risk misinterpreting God's word if we simply apply such teachings out of the context to other situations, without first asking if God's word to our situation has the same specific directives as those he gave (through Paul) to Corinth in 55 A.D.

Second Generation Christianity

In the widened "ripple," or second generation of Christianity, the traumatic destruction of Jerusalem put an end to the dominance of the Jerusalem church and of Jewish Christians, who had for some time been outnumbered by Gentile Christians. By this time, the original Jewish disciples of Jesus were also fast dying out.

Meanwhile, the failure of Christians to support the messianic fever which Josephus claims was an aspect of the Jewish rebellion against Rome led to ever greater alienation between Jews and Jewish Christians. In Christian communities and writings still predominately Jewish from the period after 65 A.D., such as Matthew (80s), John (latest edition, 90s but earlier layers), and Revelation (probably 90s), there is clear evidence of this alienation from Jews, persecution instigated by Jews, and competition (sometimes not very successful) against a nearby synagogue. This alienation led to actual separation and expulsion from the synagogue, also clearly attested in these writings and in the Jewish evidence of the existence of a curse against Christians inserted into the daily Jewish prayers.

As Christians and Jews went their separate ways after 70 A.D., the fight over whose scriptures were the Old Testament was heightened. This is obvious in Matthew and John. But it is also present in writings for churches where Gentile Christianity was dominant, as in Luke and Acts. One of Luke's main purposes is to show how his predominantly Gentile church can be said to be the legitimate heirs of the (Jewish) Old Testament promises and grounded in the very Jewish Jesus, apostles, and Paul. These first-century tensions between Christians and Jews need not be perpetuated in our century, as can happen if the New Testament is read without taking the historical situation into account.

As the Church moved into the second and third generations, there obviously had to be more emphasis on remembering what the earlier witnesses had taught and handed on as the tradition about Jesus. In their struggle against misrepresentations and misinterpretations of the Christian Gospel, the churches laid increasing emphasis on tracing a succession of public authority figures from the apostles to their present leaders. Leadership also was becoming standardized to the local leadership roles of bishops, elders, and deacons. For example, the turn-of-the-century *Didache* treated those roles as replacements for the wandering apostles and prophets who were dying out. Because of the danger of secret traditions among heretical gnostic groups and private revelations among millenarian groups, mainline churches began to speak of faith as belief in a deposit of traditional teaching rather than in Paul's more dynamic sense of faith as accepting God's pardon for one's sins. The theme of "false prophets" became more prominent in later-generation Christianity. At the end of the first-century, 1 John 4:2-3 contains an explicit refutation of the heresy of docetism which denied that

Jesus was truly man. The opposite heresy held by splinter groups of Jewish Christians denied the divinity of Jesus. This heresy was combatted in the second century, and the Gospels written from this standpoint were excluded from the Church's scripture.

Rather than justifying the need for a "canon within a canon," such later developments are inevitable for any group that moves beyond its original generation and inspiration into succeeding generations. The New Testament itself gives evidence for the later Church on how earliest Christianity translated its message and structures in a way that could be passed on to later generations.

After the deaths of Paul, Peter, and James, the brother of the Lord, some unknown Christians felt the need to gather into one collection copies of Paul's letters written to churches hundreds of miles apart (Asia Minor, Greece, Rome). We have seen that 2 Peter refers to some such collection and treats it in the same breath as "the other scriptures." This very act of gathering the letters and making them available to churches other than those who originally received them had the effect of making the letters more universal and less occasional. Since most of them had originally been responses to particular problems and situations, Paul's letters had a certain "scandal of particularity" about them, in that some of his discussions pertain only to the original situation.[22] Only by extension and analogy could some instructions to Corinth be applied in Rome, for example. The gathering of letters to churches in different parts of the Empire resulted in a broad sample of Paul's thought and pastoral approaches under a variety of circumstances, which by being read together could provide insights into how he might approach new problems that the current church faced.

Most scholars feel that this desire for Pauline teaching went even further after Paul's death and the death of most of the first apostles. Not only were Paul's letters collected, but later writers in the Pauline churches used these letters, his vocabulary and theology, as the foundation from which to write letters in his name after his death. They did this in order to meet current problems in a Pauline spirit. This practice of pseudonymous letter writing, totally alien to our contemporary notions of authorship, was common in the first century and was distinguished from the practice of forgery. For example, the Epicurean philosophical schools produced letters of Epicurus decades and even centuries after his death. Pseudonymous writing was a common practice in Jewish apocalyptic writing, as evidenced by the names given to works like Daniel, Enoch, the Apocalypse of Ezra, and the Apocalypse of Moses (a name for Jubilees).[23]

Raymond Brown has written in the *Jerome Biblical Commentary* a fine summary of the five kinds of biblical authorship.[24] The first type occurred when a man wrote a book in his own hand (e.g., Luke probably did this). The second consisted of dictating a letter to a scribe or secretary who copied slavishly (e.g., some of Paul's letters). Both of these would be called authorship in our sense today. The third type of authorship was attributed to a man who supplied the basic ideas for a "ghost writer" who would then write in his own words. Today we usually acknowledge the "ghost writer" by the phrase, "as told to," though some businessmen commission expert secretaries to compose a letter for them, to which they affix their own signature. Papal encyclicals are often composed in this way, and the "ghost writers" are not acknowledged. If the letter of James dates back to James, the Galilean relative of Jesus, it would seem to have had to have been ghost-written. For it is written in the most refined Greek found in the New Testament, which seems unlikely for a Galilean whose first language was Aramaic and who probably would not have received much more training in Greek than Jesus did.

The fourth type of authorship is what we today clearly call pseudonymous: a man was considered the author if his disciples wrote guided by his teaching, his expressions, and his spirit (even if long after the master's death). Parts of Isaiah and Jeremiah, probably some of the Johannine corpus, and perhaps Matthew and 2 Peter exemplify this type of authorship by disciples. Most scholars consider the pastoral letters of Paul to be of this type, though many would insist that genuine Pauline passages (like the request for his cloak and books) are incorporated too. Scholars debate whether Ephesians, Colossians,

2 Thessalonians, and the catholic epistles fall into the category of pseudonymous authorship.

The fifth type of biblical authorship is farthest from our modern meaning. A man could be considered the author if the book was written in the literary tradition for which he was famous. Thus David is said to be author of all the psalms, Solomon of all the wisdom writings, Moses of all the Pentateuch, even though parts of these writings were not produced until centuries after their deaths.

Since the Church no longer insists that the apostolic authorship of New Testament books be maintained, there is no problem in faith with accepting what at least in many cases are the legitimate conclusions of careful scholarly investigation about the pseudonymity of several New Testament books.[25] In this case, inspiration applies to the disciple who composed the letter in his master's name and honor. By doing this the disciple is saying that if Paul were here today, this is how he would answer this problem in our church.

One kind of New Testament writing that is consistently misunderstood and misinterpreted is the eschatological prediction of Jesus' speedy return. Contrary to many theories about the "delay of the parousia" and the Church going stagnant and settling down for "the long haul," many of the later New Testament books are the most emphatic in expecting the parousia very soon, such as Revelation and 2 Peter. (For that matter, Justin Martyr in 150 A.D. was just as expectant). Instead of discouraging the early Christians, the delay occasioned explanations of why the parousia had not yet come about (Luke-Acts) and assurances that it would not be much longer (2 Peter). Today we have to admit that this widespread expectation that Jesus would return in the lifetimes of the first Christians (an expectation common to most of the New Testament and found in sayings attributed to Jesus) was mistaken in its timing. We still believe that the parousia will come, but the Church refuses to put a date on it. Since the later Fathers, it has discouraged millennialism, and forbids it to be taught, even though it originates in a straightforward literal reading of Rv 20:1-6.[26] The human limitations of the New Testament authors are seen in this example of an almost universal expectation that did not in fact come true. Even in the New Testament there are dissenting voices forbidding the calculation of times and seasons (e.g., Acts 1:6). Vatican II deals indirectly with such problems by insisting that the truth of scripture is truth needed for our salvation (*salutis causa* — *On Revelation*, Art. 11). Our salvation does not depend on knowing when the End will come. It does depend on the fact that Jesus is the Son of God, who died for our sins, is Lord and eschatological Judge.

It is only toward the end of the second century that most of the New Testament books were considered by the Church to be scripture, but the margins remained fuzzy, with books like *The Shepherd of Hermas* included in some churches and New Testament books like *Revelation* excluded in others.[27] The slowness of this process of canonizing the New Testament is a fine illustration of the need, not only for "the Bible and Jesus," but for the Church as well. The first-century Church did not yet have the New Testament. It did have the preaching of the Apostles to the community.

Conclusion

Vatican II asked exegetes to discover the meaning which the human authors of scripture intended when they wrote and the situations within which they wrote as a help in understanding and explaining the meaning of scripture. The Council views this as preparatory study by which the judgment of the Church (the final interpreter of scripture) may mature (*On Revelation*, Art. 12). It is in this spirit that I submit this study of the historical origins of the Church and New Testament writings as evidence for understanding what is meant by inspiration of the New Testament. Knowledge of how the writings came to be written and gathered brings out the implications of the statement, "The Bible is the word of God in words of men."

The first implication resulting from our study is that the inspiration of the New Testament should be understood as part of the larger process of God's guidance of his growing Church.

The complicated nature of the process of writing, gathering, editing, and selecting the New Testament writings, which finally resulted in our canon of 27 books, requires a sophisticated view of God's inspiration, which extends far beyond the kind of explicit guiding of individual authors found in Revelation. It must also apply to the preaching, oral traditions, and early stages of the material now present in the New Testament as well as to its gathering, editing, and later additions (e.g., the ending in Mk 16:9-20). It does not seem necessary to suppose that every author e.g., Luke, actually was aware of himself as being inspired by God when he wrote. At first, little was written down, and even in most of that, such as Paul's letters and collections of the sayings of Jesus, the evidence points more to the writer's consciousness of meeting a need in the churches rather than of being "inspired" to write scripture on the same level with the Old Testament.

Later parts of the New Testament provide evidence that, after a period of primarily oral teaching and tradition, there arose in many places a need to gather and preserve for later generations the witness, teaching, and examples of early witnesses and church leaders. Thus the Gospel writers gathered into unified accounts many of the early traditions about Jesus. Acts includes numerous traditions about the first missionaries and churches. Collectors of Paul's letters and writers of pseudonymous letters in the name of apostles wanted to preserve and apply apostolic teaching and examples for later situations as the first generation was dying out. In this case, much of God's inspiration seems to pertain to the act of gathering, updating, and applying earlier church traditions in new writings, like Gospels or pseudonymous letters, or in new collections of old writings, such as Paul's letters.

Again, the context of inspiration is thoroughly ecclesial — within and for the Church. We are not dealing with hermits who were inspired to write messages for other isolated individuals. Even in Revelation, the example that seems most like this, the prophet John was writing as an exile from his churches; was inspired as he prayed in spiritual union with them during the time they were meeting on the Lord's Day; and wrote to and for the churches as a prophet whose authority was recognized by those churches. In every single case, the New Testament writings were written for the churches and were the responsibility of those churches to preserve, teach, and interpret. They were never meant to be used independently from the Christian churches, as God's direct channel of revelation to isolated individuals.

A related implication has to do with the fact that, well into the second century, Christians were completely dependent on the teaching in the churches and whatever New Testament writings each church possessed. No complete New Testament was available. The writings now included in our New Testament existed alongside other writings which later were rejected from the canon. Nor before the printing press was invented in the late 1400s was there any possibility that all Christians could have their own copy of the Bible. The notion that each Christian can find his or her own way to God with just the Bible and without any church ties was simply impossible to hold before the printing press made Bibles inexpensive and easy to duplicate. For the first 1400 years of Christianity, it was obvious to everyone that God's word in the scripture was available to individuals only as members of the Church. God's word in scripture was preserved and copied in the Church and preached, taught, and interpreted in the Church. Before the printing press, God's word could never appear to be independent from the Church.

Even after all the New Testament books were written, the churches continued to have to preserve them, make them available to the people (usually by reading them to the assembly), and select their canon of scripture. That is, from among many writings, the churches had to determine which were the authentic word of God and distinguish them from pious and helpful writings that were not scripture and from still other writings which were actually heretical or harmful to authentic Christian faith and morality. The historical facts show that it was the Church that was solely responsible for selecting and fixing the canon of scripture. We believe this too happened under God's guidance.

But there can be no doubt that scripture was given to the

Church. It is God's word to the Church and to individuals as members of the Church. Thus it is still the responsibility of the Church today, as it was in the first centuries, to teach the word of God, and to judge between authentic and inauthentic interpretations of this word. The Church must both submit in obedience to God's word, and correct Christians or others who misinterpret God's word. This is one reason why the division of the Church into competing denominations is so scandalous. That division renders this task of the Church to oversee the authentic interpretation and teaching of God's word almost impossible. Also, since scripture belongs to the Church, scholars as scholars cannot be the final arbiters of the meaning of scripture as the word of God, nor can individual Christians in isolation from Christ's Body exercise this function, no matter how prayerfully they read the Bible. The nature of scripture as the Church's scripture (as the Koran is the Mohammedan scripture and the Vedas are Hindu scripture) excludes both the arrogance of scholars who would ignore or even spurn the faith of the Church in their interpretation and the individualism of those who would use the Bible as their own private channel to God without any sense of obedience to those God put in authority.

Finally, the situational aspect of inspiration we have described has important implications for how one interprets and applies scripture today. God's word to an unjust people as found in Amos consisted of harsh condemnation and a demand for change. His word to discouraged exiles in the latter part of Isaiah was hope and comfort. It would be misusing scripture to use those comfort texts to reinforce false complacency in a lukewarm community today. The diverse aspects of God's word are all meant for corresponding situations.

Similarly, our findings about the Christian-Jewish tensions in the initial separation of the two groups warn us that some parts of the New Testament reflect a hostility that must not be directed toward innocent Jews today. The horrible lesson of the Nazi persecution of Jews should warn us to be careful of letting anti-Semitism be legitimized by New and even Old Testament texts. On the other hand, promises in Jewish writings of both the Old and New Testament about Jerusalem, Zion, or return to the promised land cannot be uncritically applied to contemporary Zionism or the issue between Jews and Arabs in Israel. Reading texts out of their historical context can do great damage.

The same kind of caution has to be applied to specific biblical directives, even in the New Testament. God's inspiration did not prevent writers from writing down their time-conditioned and cultural prejudices, as in some of the slighting New Testament references to women and their roles. Though it might seem so much easier and safer simply to "do what the Bible says" in such matters, we can never be excused from thinking fully about the application even of an inspired text from another cultural era to our own age. The examples of anti-Semitism, subordination of women, and the obvious one of slavery are just some of those that could be cited to show the need, not only to know what scripture says about a topic, but also how to apply that scriptural evidence today (through systematic, moral, or pastoral theology or preaching). Since God has chosen to reveal his message in the words of men, complete with the limitations of those words, we have no recourse but to use the human talents and resources which God has given to us, along with the guidance of his Spirit, to study the human aspects of his word and discover how it is to be applied to our own times.

USING THE
SCRIPTURES FOR PRAYER

Paul Hinnebusch, O.P.

Vatican II tells us why God speaks to mankind in his revealed word: "Through this revelation, the invisible God out of the abundance of his love speaks to men as friends and lives among them, so that he may invite and take them into friendship with himself" (Dei Verbum 2).

Friendship between God and man is the whole purpose of God's word of revelation. God speaks to his friends and invites a response. Only if there is a response can the friendship be established and maintained. This response is prayer. As God continues to speak through his word, and his friends continue to respond, a loving communion is established and deepened. This loving communion is a fullness of prayer.

Since loving response to God is prayer, let us see some qualities this response should have if it is to qualify as prayer.

A Response to a Person

The response to God's word should be a response to a Person present with us, speaking his word. When the scriptures are heard or read in faith, they are like a sacrament of God's presence. They are sign and instrument of his personal presence and communion with us. In the scriptures we meet God himself and we meet Jesus his Son, in the Holy Spirit.

This truth is strikingly expressed in the story of the disciples of Emmaus (Lk 24:13-35). The risen Lord was truly present with the disciples as they walked with him along the road, though they did not recognize him. He was present in their hearts, enlightening them from within by the Holy Spirit, opening their hearts to understand the scriptures. Though God was with them and speaking to them, they came to the full awareness of his presence only later when they reflected back on the experience. "Did not our hearts burn within us while he talked to us on the road, while he opened to us the scriptures?" (Lk 24:32).

So too when we hear or read the scriptures, our hearts often burn within us, without our reflecting on what is happening, without our realizing that we are in communion with a living Person who is working in our hearts by an interior word of grace. Our listening to the scriptures, or our reading them, is already a prayer, for our hearts, responding to the word, are responding to a Person present with us through his word and Spirit.

We can be touched by the Lord through the scriptures without even adverting to the fact that we are being touched. We can be praying in response to the scriptures without even knowing that we are praying. Indeed, some of the very best prayer is the unselfconscious prayer that takes place in the persons of childlike simplicity who never stand back to look at themselves to see how well they are praying.

Prayer is a response to God and communion with him in faith, hope, and love. Just to seek God through the scriptures in faith, hope, and love is prayer. Love's desire for God is already prayer, for it is a reaching out, an opening of self to him for deeper communion with him. Reading God's word with faith and love brings forth a new response in faith and love, and this new response is prayer, whether we realize we are praying or not.

The insight which comes as we read the scriptures with faith is a quickening of faith. This quickened faith is itself a prayerful response to the word. The joyful acceptance of this new insight is prayer, for it is a loving response to the Person who is present to us through his word.

Fullness of Response

Our response to God's word frequently contains elements of resistance, a lack of generous response, a questioning or doubting. These elements partly or wholly vitiate our prayer, for they weaken or destroy our loving response to the God who is speaking to us.

Sometimes our response is an honest questioning that seeks further enlightenment. A response of total acceptance presupposes some understanding of what it is to which we are asked to respond. Thus Mary did not hesitate to ask Gabriel, the messenger of God's word, "How can this be, since I do not know man?" (Lk 1:34). It was not a question of doubt but of sincere seeking. When she was further enlightened by the word of God, her response was total: "I am the servant of the Lord. Let it be done to me as you say" (Lk 1:38).

Thus our scriptural prayer is sometimes a real dialogue with God but it needs to culminate in a full response, a complete yielding of self to the Lord in loving communion.

When we see how the people in scripture respond to the Lord in loving faith and adoration, a similar response springs forth from our hearts. We watch Thomas as he responds to the risen Lord, saying, "My Lord and my God!" (Jn 20:28), and the same response comes forth from our heart. This is prayer. We listen as Peter makes his great act of faith, "You are the Messiah, the Son of the living God" (Mt 16:16), and the same act of faith springs forth from our heart. This is prayer. We look at Peter as he commits himself to Jesus in complete trust and hopeful expectation, saying, "Lord, to whom shall we go? You have the words of eternal life" (Jn 6:68), and the same act of hope wells up from our heart. This is prayer. We hear Peter repeat three times, "Lord, you know that I love you" (Jn 21:15), and our heart cries out the same words of love. This is prayer. This is faith, hope, and love bringing us into communion with God in the Holy Spirit.

Pondering the Word

The memory of scriptural scenes like these remains with us, and, like Mary, we continue to ponder them in our hearts (Lk 2:19, 51). We continue to pray, to respond in faith and love to the Lord, who dwells with us in these scenes presented in his word. That is what we do in that great scriptural prayer, Our Lady's Rosary. Day after day as we pray the mysteries, we respond anew to the Lord in the way that Mary did, in the way that Elizabeth did.

As we ponder the mystery of the Annunciation, for example, our heart cries out with Mary, "I am the servant of the Lord" (Lk 1:38). As we ponder the mystery of the Visitation, with Elizabeth we cry out to welcome Mary and the Son whom she carries in her womb, "Blest are you among women, and blest is the fruit of your womb!" (Lk 1:42). The Lord Jesus is present to us through his Holy Spirit as we ponder the Rosary mysteries, and in the Holy Spirit we respond to him in faith and loving trust. This is an outstanding way of using the scriptures for prayer.

As we joyfully accept this continuing presence of God manifested to us in the scriptures, our relationship with the Lord is deepened. The various types of relationships with him depicted in the scriptures are fashioned in our hearts by the Holy Spirit. Like the tax-collector, for example, we respond to the Lord in humble contrition, "O God, be merciful to me, a sinner" (Lk 18:13). Or with Jesus in his agony, we submit our will to the Father in a struggling prayer, "Not my will, but yours be done" (Lk 22:42).

Through the prayerful faith and loving trust which is drawn from our hearts by the scriptures, we are opened to the Lord's presence and his loving action in our hearts. We come into ever-deepening communion with him. As we thus focus our lives and our attention on the Lord who is ever with us, even unreflectively we begin to imitate what we see and love in him. Thus not just our thoughts and our desires, but our whole being enters into a loving relationship with him. The word of God forms our whole life into the likeness of the Word himself.

Praying the Scriptures in the Psalms

The psalms are a perfect way of praying the Bible, for they are an inspired response to the rest of God's revelation, the revelation of himself in salvation deeds and in words.[1] (I have treated this topic in detail in *Praise: A Way of Life*, 1976.)

As a source of daily biblical prayer, we can also use the liturgical responses to the scripture readings in the Mass and in the liturgy of the hours. We can reflect on the reading, and then reflect on the psalm-response, trying to see how it responds precisely to the particular word of the reading, and how that response is needed in our own life.

The Scriptures as Symbols or Mysteries

"Did not our hearts burn within us while he talked to us on the way, while he opened to us the scriptures?" (Lk 24:32). The risen Lord is usually working in our hearts for some time before we realize what is happening. Then suddenly we realize that the scriptures are speaking about what he is doing in our hearts, and through the scriptures we come to understand his action in us. Usually we can respond to the scriptures only because we have some degree of prereflective experience of his action in our hearts, the action of which the scriptures speak. We find that the scriptures put into words what the Lord is doing in us in a wordless way. Only because he is working these realities in our hearts, through his Holy Spirit, do we understand what the scriptures are saying.

The reality which the Lord is accomplishing in our hearts in a wordless way is a reality too big for words. Words and ideas, even the inspired biblical words, are inadequate to express it fully. The scriptural words, and the events they present, are not always precise descriptions of God's work in our hearts; they are symbols of something which is too great to define and confine in words. They symbolize for us what God wishes to do in us through our response. The traditional name for the scriptures as symbols is "mysteries."

A symbol stands for a reality which is too great to be

contained and described in mere ideas and words. The symbol helps us to identify with the reality it symbolizes. The word "symbol" derives from Greek words (*syn* + *ballein*) meaning "to throw together," "to compare." Two parts of one reality are compared. Our identity with the reality is verified when we see ourselves in the symbol which represents the reality.

For example, the story of the signing of the American Declaration of Independence becomes a symbol of the whole reality of the independent American nation. Again and again we tell the story of the Declaration of Independence to celebrate our identity with the reality which began on that historical occasion. We identify with that event because we are a living part of the reality which began with it.

A more glorious identification and participation takes place when we tell or read again the scriptural accounts of God's saving action in human history. For in this case, the same God who acted in person in the presence of the apostles is still present with us in full reality, continuing in us the same saving action he accomplished in them. We can identify with the reality expressed in the symbol, the mystery, the scriptural event, because this Lord is actively present with us, working that reality in us.

The scriptures as symbols or mysteries, then, help us to identify with the reality they represent. We truly share in the reality spoken of in the scriptures. This is the ever-continuing reality of God's true and loving presence with mankind. In Christ, he offers himself to us, saves us, shares his life with us, and invites us into loving communion with him. St. Paul sums it up when he says that God's "word in its fullness" is "the mystery of Christ in you, your hope of glory" (Col 1:25, 27). The words and events of the scriptures are mysteries manifesting the divine reality of God's presence, which is too great for words.

The scriptural accounts as symbols show forth the reality strikingly without adequately expressing it in words or ideas, for it infinitely surpasses words. The symbol or mystery is like a sacrament of this reality: it is a sign and instrument of God's saving presence with us. When the scriptural mystery comes alive for us, when our hearts burn within us, when we vibrate with it, we are responding to the living presence of the Lord himself, not just to words. We are able to identify with the mysteries because they show forth the reality which the Lord is working in our hearts. The Lord is continuing among us the saving action described in the scriptural words and events. His words to the doubting Thomas, for example, "Do not be unbelieving, but believing," are his words to me, and I respond to them in the way Thomas did, "My Lord and my God!"

The symbol draws and captures our hearts. It enables us to enter into the reality it expresses, into the Lord's saving presence. The mysteries speak to us in a moving way because, along with them, the Lord speaks in our hearts the interior word of his presence.

The response to the scriptural word is authentic only to the extent that the Lord is actually accomplishing in our hearts the reality of which the scriptures are speaking. Our "Amen" to the reality of which they speak is possible only because we somehow know in our hearts the truth which they express. And we know it in our hearts because God is working it in a wordless way by the grace of his presence.

Thus we come to an understanding of the scriptures only because, somehow, we are experiencing in our hearts what the scriptures are talking about. We come to an understanding of what God is doing in our hearts because we begin to realize that the scriptures are speaking of the very thing he is doing in us. This new realization is an encouraging confirmation of what God is doing. It enables us to respond more fully to our wordless experience, of which, perhaps, we were hardly aware. It brings the joy of knowing we are on the right track and that God is with us. It invites a new, deeper, and more conscious response to his presence and action. In the new response, the reality is deepened within us. This new response is truly prayer, for it brings us into deeper communion with God.

Specific Response to the Word

Though the reality symbolized in the scriptures is too great to be adequately articulated even in divinely inspired words, the response that the scriptures call forth to this reality is not vague and inarticulate. For the invisible, inaccessible God has made himself accessible, visible, audible, tangible, present in the Person of the Word-made-flesh, who remains with us always as risen Lord. The scriptures tell us of this presence and show forth in a tangible, visible, audible way the mystery of God-with-us, a reality which infinitely surpasses understanding. They give precious, if partial, insights into God's "word in its fullness... the mystery of Christ in you." Thus they do draw forth a specific response from our hearts to the living God.

In different passages the Lord highlights different aspects of the mystery, and thus calls forth from our hearts different kinds of response. The specific way in which we respond is conditioned by what the ever-present Lord is offering us in a particular passage.

Sometimes when we read his scriptures, he simply offers his presence to us to be loved and enjoyed. Read the story of the Magi, and with the Magi fall down and worship the Christ Child. Remain as long as possible in his presence, simply rejoicing in his love and growing in prayerful communion with him.

In some passages, the ever-present Lord shows to me the conditions which I must fulfill for living in his presence: "As the Father has loved me, so have I loved you. Live on in my love. You will live in my love if you keep my commandments, even as I have kept my Father's commandments and live in his love" (Jn 15:9).

Sometimes he speaks to us a word of vocation. St. Anthony the Hermit, for example, received his call from God one day at Mass when he heard the Lord speak directly to his heart the words of the scriptures, "if you want to be perfect, go and sell all you have and give the money to the poor, and you will have riches in heaven. Then come and follow me." Anthony's response was immediate and complete.

Sometimes he gives us through the scriptures the light we need for making a particular decision or the answer to a question we are asking. St. Therese of Lisieux had been confused about her role in the Body of Christ, the Church. She searched the scriptures for an answer. God spoke to her heart through the twelfth and thirteenth chapters of Corinthians. She did not recognize herself in the various members of Christ's body of which Paul speaks there — apostles, prophets, teachers, and so forth. But as she went on to read Paul's great description of love, she realized that the Body of Christ, made up of so many different members, needs a heart aflame with love. Thus she found her own place in this Body: "In the heart of the Church my Mother, I will be love."

It is right that we should search the scriptures in this way for answers to our questions. A friend whom I had recently received into the Catholic Church had an infant daughter. Because of the strong Baptist influences in his life, this man was unable to accept infant baptism for his child. I felt a strong responsibility to help him accept this, since I had received him into the Church. But my words of explanation were of no avail. The man's personal experience of adult baptism had been so glorious that he felt he must not deprive his daughter of an experience that only an adult could have. But he sincerely wanted to do God's will and searched the scriptures for the answer, which he could not accept from me. One day in prayer, the Lord led him to open the scriptures to the words, "Let the children come to me, do not hinder them; for to such belongs the kingdom of God" (Mark 10:14). God spoke to his heart through these words, convincing him that the child should be baptized.

Sometimes without even opening the scriptures or listening to them proclaimed in the liturgy, we hear God speak them clearly in our hearts in answer to our needs. A friend tells how she had lost her mother when she was still a little child, and therefore she never had a mother at the time when she really needed one. Some months after her wedding, when her marriage seemed to be breaking up, she desperately felt the need of a mother to help her in this situation. She had been raised in the Baptist religion, and so it never occurred to her to go to Mary, the Mother of Jesus. She did go to Jesus. As she prayed, Jesus vividly spoke to her the words of the scriptures, "Behold your mother" (Jn 19:27). She responded and accepted Mary as her mother and found the help she needed. She said that it was like Jesus, the man, saying to her: "I was never a woman, I was never a mother. I give you my mother to be your mother, for she has experienced the motherhood which I have not experienced."

Men in the Church need to listen to women in the Church, for women can experience aspects of the mystery of Christ which men cannot. Men and women need to listen to one another, male leaders in the Church need to take counsel with women, especially in matters which concern women.

This woman, who needed a mother so desperately, experienced in depth the mystery symbolized in the words of John's Gospel which speak of Mary at the foot of the cross, accepting as her son the disciple whom Jesus loved (Jn 19:25-27). The woman's living experience opened her heart to understand that the disciple whom Jesus loved is a symbol of every true believer. Jesus invites every believer to accept his mother as his own.

In a similar way, many other scriptural accounts symbolize divine realities which escape the understanding of those who have had no experience of the reality. The story of the Visitation (Lk 1:39-45), for example, is the mystery or symbol of Mary's power in the Holy Spirit to visit each one of us, of her power in the Holy Spirit to be in communion with us as our spiritual mother, just as she was in communion with Elizabeth in that same Holy Spirit. Her presence with Elizabeth was no mere human presence; it was a presence in the Holy Spirit, who had filled her and who now filled Elizabeth so that she could recognize Mary as Mother of the Lord.

Only those who have experienced Mary's presence with them in the Holy Spirit know that this scriptural story presents the mystery of Mary's presence with Christians everywhere. From early youth as I have prayed the Rosary, I have never hesitated to respond to this mystery by inviting Mary to visit me, opening my heart in faith to her presence. To be in her presence in this way, one does not need to have some sense-perceptible experience. It is enough to know in faith that she is there wherever she is invited, and even where she is not invited. She herself takes the initiative to be with us, in fulfillment of her maternal responsibility for us.

It is to be expected that many of God's people will hear the words of the scriptures addressed personally to them, since the whole message of the scriptures is God's real presence with us, acting in our hearts with his saving power. We should be slow to doubt when people tell us that God has spoken his scriptural words to their hearts. The whole purpose of scripture is to touch each person for whom Christ died, just as God in Christ spoke directly to the hearts of his disciples.

Unselfconscious Response to the Word

People often say to me in disappointment, "I never get words from the Lord when I read the scriptures. When I pray for guidance, the scriptures never come alive for me with an answer to my problem. It never seems that the Lord is speaking a passage directly to me." Yet when I pursue the matter with these people, many times it becomes clear that they have been prayerfully responding to the Lord in the scriptures for years. Usually this has been in a completely unselfconscious way. The Lord has spoken his word in their hearts, and without reflecting on what has been happening, they have responded to his various words, calling for repentance, love, faith, trust, or the like. They have responded, thinking no more of it than a fish thinks about the water in which he swims, no more than one thinks about the air he breathes. They have been "at home" with the Lord, much as a little child is at home with his loving parents in unreflective simplicity, completely open to their influence, and responding to them without realizing that he is doing so. People who have this kind of simple, unselfconscious faith are often more genuine than some of the people who are always claiming to have words from the Lord.

It is not necessary that the word frequently come alive for us in a very vivid way. Most of the time it is enough for us to read the scriptures faithfully and to respond unselfconsciously in faith and love, letting the Lord do his work in our hearts in an unperceived way.

Each time we use the scriptures for prayer, we need not expect a particular word concerning a mission we are to accomplish, a project we are to undertake, a virtue we are to practice, or the answer to a problem. The Lord most often simply offers his presence to us, to be accepted with love and joy, in faith and trust. Most of the time the word he speaks to us is a word of love and communion, rather than a word entrusting us with a great mission or a glamorous service to be rendered.

Not that the words of mission do not come, but they are rarer than the words of quiet communion. The people who are always looking for vivid words of mission or action tend to miss the delicate words of interior communion, the interior word of grace.

Because they miss the interior word of silent communion, some people play "biblical roulette," repeatedly seeking a word from God by "cutting the pages" of the scriptures. The person who is accustomed to loving communion with God in quiet faith usually finds this sort of thing unnecessary. This is not to deny that God sometimes does speak in this way to people when they honestly seek an answer from him in humble sincerity of heart. We have already insisted that it is to be expected that God's people will often hear the words of scripture addressed to them personally, especially in the liturgy. But we are warning against forcing the word by playing the what has been called "biblical roulette." Sometimes God may prefer that we listen to his "wordless" presence in total trust that he is working in our lives, whether we are fully aware of what he is doing or not.

The word of scripture, we said, is intended above all to bring us into intimate communion with God. With it comes the interior word which is God's presence, the indwelling Word in Person who communicates wordlessly with us through his presence in our hearts. This is "his word in its fullness...the mystery of Christ in you" (Col 1:25, 27). This is the deeper reality which the scriptural words themselves cannot adequately express. The words are but symbols opening us to this unspeakable Presence. Sometimes the only adequate response to this Presence is loving adoration and wordless self-surrender to him. And if the Presence does not cause our hearts to burn within us, at least we respond to him in quiet waiting and expectant hope, ready to receive his self-manifestation if and when he sees fit to give it. It cannot be forced. It is the free gift of love.

Experience beyond Exegesis

Because the reality symbolized in the scriptures is too big for words, we should not be surprised if people sometimes experience God speaking to them in passages in a way which seems to violate the rules of scriptural exegesis. At times God may symbolize a spiritual experience to a prayerful person through scriptural words that in their literal inspired meaning do not speak of what the person is experiencing. The person may come across a portion of scripture that seems to perfectly express a particular spiritual experience. He then uses these words to express his experience to others, even though the biblical author was not thinking of that particular experience at all when he wrote the words under divine inspiration.

When that happens, God may indeed be speaking to the person through those particular scriptural words and clarifying the experience through them. If the person tries to use these scriptures to urge his own experience upon others, or to draw theological conclusions from the words, as if his personal experience were something universally valid for everyone, problems can result. The fact that God may have used a passage in this way to speak to us personally does not mean that we must urge our interpretation of this passage upon others. Though it may be for us a true interpretation of our personal religious experience, it is not necessarily a true interpretation of the inspired meaning of the passage.

For example, a man I know was caught up into a glorious experience of the heavenly choirs of praise and found his experience strikingly symbolized in Isaiah's description of the angels loudly praising God (Is 6:3-4). The man concluded that Isaiah teaches that one should praise God by shouting at the top of his voice. However, he failed to distinguish the reality he experienced from the scriptural symbol in which he experienced it. Though his personal experience of heavenly praise was genuine, it did not follow that everyone had to experience it in that precise way.

Sometimes an experience of a spiritual reality and the symbol in which it is expressed to the understanding seem so inseparably one, that, for the person who has the experience, the symbol is the reality.

Something like this once happened to St. Catherine of Siena. Jesus appeared to her and took her heart from her breast and replaced it with his own heart. Thus, in a striking mystical symbol, God accomplished in her the reality of which he speaks through Ezekiel: "I will give you a new heart and place a new spirit within you, taking from your bodies your stony hearts and giving you natural hearts. I will put my spirit within you" (Ez 36:26-27).

The spiritual reality accomplished in this mystical experience was so vivid to Catherine that no one could ever convince her that Jesus had not literally replaced her heart with his own bodily heart. She was unable to distinguish the symbol from the divine reality which Christ accomplished in her, namely, her total transformation in his own divine love, her perfect union with him, in which she lived his own life and loved with his own love.

In the same way, my friend did not distinguish the divine reality of the heavenly liturgy from the scriptural symbol in which he experienced it, or through which he interpreted his experience. Though God may have mediated the experience to him through the imagery of that scriptural passage, this does not mean that the passage itself teaches that it is good to praise God with a loud voice.

Pastors, exegetes, and theologians should understand that this sort of experience of the scriptures can be authentic, even though it does not seem to correspond to the rules of exegesis or theological reflection.

Any spiritual experience and consequent insight into the scriptures needs to be checked against the total divine revelation and against the whole Christian experience through the centuries. No passage of the scriptures should ever be interpreted apart from the context of God's complete revelation.

A friend of mine had had some experience of miraculous physical healings granted through prayer in the name of Jesus, but she never had any experience of a Christian vocation to suffer sickness in union with Jesus. Therefore, relying only on her limited experience of physical healings through prayer, she interpreted the words, "He took our infirmities and bore our diseases" (Mt 8:17) to mean that God wills that no one should ever be sick and that anyone who is physically healed must not be "in God's will."

But another woman refuted this interpretation of that passage by appealing to her personal experience of a word from God inviting her to accept her physical infirmities as a vocation to "complete what is lacking in Christ's afflictions for the sake of his body, the Church" (Col 1:24).

No one experience of the Christian mystery exhausts that mystery. The ways of the Holy Spirit are multiple. There are many ways of expressing Christ in our lives, all of them in accord with the inspired meaning of the scriptures.

For example, perhaps someone has experienced praying in tongues as the "groanings that cannot be expressed in speech" (Rom 8:26). But this by no means exhausts the reality expressed in Paul's words. It would be wrong to insist that one who has never prayed in tongues has never experienced that reality. The reality can be experienced in a profound way as a Spirit-inspired groaning for the object of Christian hope. Paul is speaking of this hope in the context of that passage (Rom 8:24). The reality of groaning in a speechless way can be experienced not simply as prayer in tongues for this or that specific favor. That limited, specific favor, in fact, should be looked upon only as a token of the infinite reality, for which we long with unspeakable groaning, the reality which "eye has not seen, ear has not heard, nor has it so much as dawned on man, what God has prepared for those who love him" (1 Cor 2:9).

Precisely because eye has not seen nor ear heard, we do not know how to pray as we ought, and so the Spirit helps our weakness by interceding in our hearts with inexpressible longings, though we do not know exactly what we are longing for. But "He who searches the hearts knows what the Spirit means" (Rom 8:27).

Pastoral Applications

Since the mystery expressed in the scriptures is the mystery of God-with-us, revealing himself to us and offering himself in friendly communion, it should be no surprise that people of living faith sometimes experience God's word addressed to them personally. Of course we are all open to deception in these matters. People of vivid imagination and people of wishful thinking can "hear" in the scriptures what they want to hear. However, occasional deceptions and abuses like these should not lead us to conclude that everyone who tells of an experience of the word has been deceived or is a deceiver. We should not automatically doubt people when they speak of these experiences but should rather apply the common rules for discernment.

People who have received authentic words from the Lord are likely to be open to deceptive words from Satan or from their own inflated ego. Satan counterfeits words from the Lord. The scriptures show us Satan quoting scripture to Jesus himself (Mt 4). Paul warns that "even Satan disguises himself as an angel of light" (2 Cor 11:14). Paul fears that the Corinthians, who have been blessed so richly with charismatic graces, will fall away from their original faithfulness to Christ. "My fear is that just as the serpent seduced Eve by his cunning, your thoughts may be corrupted and you may fall from your sincere and complete devotion to Christ" (2 Cor 11:3).

Pride creeps stealthily into the best of us, and people who once were sincerely devoted to the Lord and truly heard his word can fall into pride and deception.

Because such falls are fairly common, priests tend to doubt every case of hearing words from the Lord. This is tragic, because it begets doubt in God's people, and kills their hope and expectation of hearing the Lord speak. After a while, no one is hearing the Lord anymore, and the scriptures are once again a sealed book. Here are a few pastoral suggestions:

1. Expect that God's word will come alive in his people. Do not let abuses by some cause you to doubt everyone.

2. Realize the limits of your own spiritual experience, and do not be surprised if God speaks to people in a way you have never experienced or calls from them a response he has never asked of you.

3. Use the normal rules for discernment of spirits.

4. Teach the people a healthy humility, a wholesome fear of deception, and a willingness to submit to the discernment of the Christian community.

5. Teach them to use personal discernment by interpreting their experiences in the context of the whole of God's revelation and in the context of the continuing experience of God's people, i.e., in the context of Christian tradition.

6. Help them to realize the diversity of God's ways and not force their personal insights upon others, who may have other valid insights, which respond to other aspects of the inexhaustible riches of Christ.

7. Help them to avoid thinking that God speaks only through the scriptures. Teach them to listen to the Christian experience of the past as well as to the scriptures. This age-old, continuing experience of the reality of which the scriptures speak — God's real presence with us to work in our hearts — gives deeper insights into the scriptures, and reveals unexpected depths of meaning in them. Much of the Church's best understanding of the scriptures is the result of reflection upon her Christian experience through the centuries. The fruit of this experience and this reflection is expressed in Christian tradition, which helps us to discern the deeper meaning of the scriptures.

HERMENEUTICS AND THE TEACHING OF SCRIPTURE

George T. Montague, S.M.

In some theological manuals — and even in Lonergan's *Method in Theology* — a distinction is made between hermeneutics and communication, the former occurring early in the theological process as an interpretation of gathered data and the latter at the end of the process as a communication of what has been understood. And yet, would not most of us agree that teaching is more than an exercise in communication, that it also has an important heuristic rebound and hermeneutical function? To teach is to expose oneself to questions one had not thought of in one's own research, questions deriving often from a world different from ours. If some of these questions are requests for completion of the hermeneutical circle opened by our exposition of the text, others are often pointers to meanings in the text itself, which we may have overlooked. Thus, the moment of teaching may prove to be a precious one even in the process of understanding the text. And so, the pedagogical question may in the long run be as important to our profession as the road performance of an automobile is to the engineering theory on which it is based.

This study was originally presented as the author's presidential address to the forty-first annual meeting of the Catholic Biblical Association of America held at the University of San Francisco August 21-24, 1978. It was originally published in the January 1979 issue of the *Catholic Biblical Quarterly* and, with minor adaptations, it is reprinted here with permission.

At any rate, the question I should like to address is this: What are the elements for an adequate method-paradigm in teaching scripture, and how should this paradigm influence teaching of specific areas? This question makes imperative the need to find a solid theoretical base, and for this we need first to ask what light can be shed on this project by recent developments in hermeneutical theory.

In Search of a Theoretical Base: Alternatives in Method

The Historical-Critical Method and Its Aftermath

It is no news to observe that the prevailing model in scriptural study and teaching today is, in one form or other, the historical-critical method. The method is used not only in the quest, old or new, of the historical Jesus, but also in form-, tradition-, and redaction-criticism, in the sense that the governing heuristic principle is the history of the text, and the presupposition of the method is that the text's meaning is that intended at the end of the process by the final author. Discovering this meaning completes the exegete's task — or so many hold — either because he is satisfied that meaning is essentially historical meaning or because he considers the hermeneutical question to be beyond his competence or his time. In practice, teaching has often stopped at this point, leaving many questions unanswered: How is this meaning to be integrated with the meaning of scripture elsewhere? What light does this throw on contemporary experience? How might the insight be lived today?

Theologians, to whom this hermeneutical task has been passed, have often found themselves ill-prepared to assess the complex biblical topography[1] and have complained that biblical scholars have not been helpful enough in this regard.[2] Homilists, in their turn, do not always find the abundance of critical material in the commentaries immediately helpful to their task, so that complaints about the hermeneutical gap have multiplied. All of this despite the high credibility given to the method in such church documents as *Divino Afflante Spiritu* and the

Constitution on Divine Revelation of the Second Vatican Council.[3]

Now voices of complaint are being heard not only from the conservative evangelical side[4] but even from among those long-exercised in the method, as, for example, J.A. Barr, A. Wilder, O.C. Edwards, A. Paul, H. Cazelles, P. Stuhlmacher, to mention only a few.[5] Walter Wink began his attack on the method with the defiant cry: "Historical biblical criticism is bankrupt."[6] By bankrupt, he meant precisely that it is no longer able to accomplish its avowed purpose which he understands thus: "so to interpret the scriptures that the past becomes alive and illumines our present with new possibilities for personal and social transformation."[7] Of the five reasons Wink gives why biblical criticism as practiced has become insolvent, I would like to comment briefly on three because I find them helpful cautions in appropriating whatever positive elements the historical method may offer for our teaching paradigm.

First, the method as practiced was incommensurate with the intention of the texts. By this he means that the supposed detached neutrality does not at all correspond to the intention of the writers to evoke or augment faith in their readers. He points out what many recent thinkers have observed, that the supposed "objective viewpoint" is none other than the historically conditioned place where the student happens to be standing and possesses no neutrality or detachment at all.[8]

Second, biblical criticism became cut off from any community for whose life its results might be significant.[9] Though in a different context, this very point was made by no less a leader in theological education and practitioner of the historical-critical method than Krister Stendahl, Dean of the Harvard Divinity School, in his convocation address two years ago:

> It has been noted, I think rightly, that the major independent and university-centered divinity schools in the U.S. have lost touch with these communities of faith. While this development had both understandable and beneficial aspects at one time — asserting the freedom from ecclesiastical interference, etc. — I believe that we have reached a point where this type

of "freedom" becomes counter-productive for all concerned, both for the universities and for the communities of faith. . . . As a divinity school we cannot be responsible in our work if we lose our roots in the communities of faith and place ourselves above or over against the communities of faith in our land.[10]

Third, biblical criticism developed in a historical context which has now changed. The historical context was polemical and apologetic. Richard Simon used historical criticism to undermine Protestant dependency on the Bible as the sole source of authority. Reimarus used it to assault the historical basis of Christianity itself. Many used it to tear down the scaffolding of a one-sided theological use of scripture, to do more justice to the individual units and their historical contexts. To conclude with Wink's crisp prose:

> Today, however, that war is largely over, and biblical critical scholarship has become the established status quo. Now the unconscious ideological elements in its position have become visible. And the unhappy consequence of this unmasking is not just that liberal biblical scholarship also proves to have been ideological, but that it has ceased to be utopian, and no longer moves toward a greater comprehension of truth. It is as if, at the moment of its victory, it had forgotten why it had fought, and settled down on the field of battle to inventory its weapons in hope of discovering some clue as to their future usefulness. Here, as in other revolutions, those who were fit to overthrow were not fit to govern.[11]

Wink's critique is, I believe, typical of those who find fault with the historical-critical method. In the last analysis, it is not against the method as such that the criticism is directed (the critics, like Wink himself, continue to use it), but only towards two points in its practice: (1) the underlying residue of historical positivism which it still often reflects; and (2) the unwillingness of its practitioners to risk moving in the direction of a hermeneutic—which amounts to a tacit acceptance of the same historical positivism.

There have been historical critics on the scene for a long time, of course, for whom the hermeneutical question has been central. One thinks immediately of Rudolf Bultmann and his efforts to salvage the New Testament kerygma via an existentialist interpretation.[12] In their own ways, Barth and Tillich sought a hermeneutic. Accepting the negative results of New Testament historical research, they evolved a theology or a metaphysics which bypassed a dependence on history. The post-Bultmannians sought a new hermeneutic by a rehabilitation of the positive results of historical inquiry, a broader understanding of the nature of history, and a theory of language as word-event. These interpretative systems, however, have been far from winning universal support, so that the only consensus among biblical experts is the continuing common *praxis* of the historical-critical method, with the limitations to which it is vulnerable. The accompanying dissatisfaction, however, signals one stage of what T.S. Kuhn has described as "normal science." For Kuhn, normal science works on the basis of a commonly accepted paradigm. Revolution in science occurs when scientists find the old paradigm increasingly inadequate to cope with anomalies and some become converted to a new paradigm, though theses under the old continue to proliferate.[13]

I would submit that one reason for the reluctance of so many historical critics to rally to the hermeneutic of Bultmann or Barth or Tillich or the post-Bultmannians or any other is the fear that the text itself is being abandoned in favor of a philosophy. Yet if a hermeneutical theory were available that emerged more directly from the text, would it have greater chance of acceptance? I do not know. But I think it significant that Norman Perrin toward the end of his life confessed that "The problem of the strength and the limitations of historical criticism, its relevance and irrelevance for the hermeneutical task, is one with which we are clearly going to have to wrestle."[14] And indeed he began to wrestle with it in his last book, which reflects the significant influence of the literary theory of Paul Ricoeur.[15]

Ricoeur accepts structuralism as a method of interpretation, though he disagrees with some of the presuppositions of structuralism as an ideology.[16] His theory does emerge out of a consideration of language and text in themselves. Whether or not the majority of historical critics will be converted to his paradigm, certainly if we are in search of fundamental elements for teaching scripture, we must look at what an elemental structural method has to offer.

Structural Exegesis and the Literary Theory of Paul Ricoeur

In contrast to the historical-critical method, which is the reconstructing of a historical process, structural exegesis presupposes a linguistic paradigm, that is, "that expression in language is to be taken as a fundamental category and not as an access to something else, e.g., history."[17]

Any text is subject to three levels of structures or constraints. (1) The structures of *enunciation*, that is, constraints imposed upon the discourse by the author and the situation he wishes to address. (2) *Cultural* structures or codes, namely the constraints that characterize a given culture. (3) The *deep structures*, which every individual seems to presuppose and which are buried in the unconscious of human beings *qua* human. Since these transcend any particular age or culture, they are called *achronic*, and in reference to them the *diachronic* methods of the historian are not necessary. These deep structures are the primary objects of structural studies.[18]

Viewed from the specifically semantic side of the question, which is Ricoeur's primary interest, the structures exist in language itself, and thus the text alone is sufficient to convey meaning. The author's intention, the addressees, and even the particular historical situation which occasioned the text are extrinsic, unnecessary and even at times obstructive to the discovery of the meaning of the text.[19]

It was the great Romanticist claim, with Schleiermacher taking the lead, that the aim of hermeneutics was to enter the subjectivity of the author himself.[20] Though refined over decades of discussion, this principle is still foundational to the historical-critical method in the often reaffirmed goal of discovering the original author's intention. However, as Ricoeur points out:

> The Romanticist forms of hermeneutics overlooked the specific situation created by the disjunction of the verbal meaning of the text from the intention of the author. . . . The surpassing of the intention by the meaning signifies precisely that understanding takes place in a non-psychological and properly semantical space, which the text has carved out by severing itself from the mental intention of the author.[21]

In other words, there is a *distantiation* that occurs when an author accepts the constraints of language by writing a text, so that the reference of the text is no longer directly to the author's intention but to the *world* which the language of the text itself opens up.[22] Thus, knowledge of the author's intention can enter into the process of validation, but it cannot be the only nor the absolute criterion of a valid interpretation[23] because the text itself carries a surplus of meaning beyond what the author may have intended. One recognizes immediately a similarity between Ricoeur's theory of textual meaning and the much disputed *sensus plenior* as described in Catholic hermeneutics: a meaning embedded in the text that goes beyond the consciousness of the author, a surplus of meaning which may be seen later and yet has roots in the text if not in the conscious intention of the author. The implications of Ricoeur's approach for an understanding of inspiration, especially its social character embedded in common language, and the recurrent problem of the "fuller sense" are discussed by Everard C. Johnston in an interesting thesis presented to the University of Louvain last fall.[24] But the discussion goes quite beyond the limits of this paper.

In such an understanding of the text, a knowledge of the addressees is not necessarily helpful. Inasmuch as the text stands as language, Paul's letters are no less addressed to me than to the Romans or the Corinthians. "The meaning of a text is open to anyone who can read. . . since the text has escaped its author, it has also escaped its original addressee."[25]

Even the original historical reference of the text seems to fall aside, since the written word overcomes the particularity of the event and universalizes it for universal appropriation:

> Writing is the paradigmatic mediation between two word-events: a word-event engenders a new word-event under the condition of the overcoming of the event in the universality of the sense; this universality alone may generate new speech events.[26]

This summary presentation of structural exegesis and the theory of Ricoeur runs the risk of doing an injustice to both, and certainly it is too brief to provide a base for adequate evaluation. Further, the practice of structural exegesis is still in such an exploratory stage that it would be rash to attempt to judge its lasting merits. The complexity to which it is sometimes carried renders it inaccessible to the ordinary student. One thing, however, it does alert us to: that the meaning of a text may be more available to the ordinary reader than the historical exegete is willing to admit. For example, is not the meaning of the story of Zacchaeus rather obvious to him who reads? And do not exegetes themselves confess that the historical setting of a great number of the Psalms is impossible to recapture — and yet the Psalms continue to speak powerfully to Jews and Christians alike. Similarly, Dominic Crossan has said about the parable: "A parable which has to be explained is, like a joke in similar circumstances, a parable that has been ruined as a parable.[27] From this we can retain that in teaching a text, attention should be paid first of all to *what is happening in the text*, and at least a preliminary study of this can be done without recourse to its original occasion and the author s intention.

Unresolved Questions

After exposure to the historical-critical method, Bultmann, the new hermeneutic, and structuralism, I still have questions which come from my teaching experience and which I feel must be answered before an adequate paradigm can be reconstructed.

Continuity and Discontinuity. The terms used in much of the philosophical elaboration of what happens when the world cf the word (or of the text) meets my world all denote discontinuity, apparently suggesting that only discontinuity is the mark of transcendence, and only by total conversion am I led to a new "self-understanding" — or whatever. My response at this point might be quibbling, but I believe that if we are speaking of the experience of faith in the New Testament context, though discontinuity is the chief element in initial conversion, there is an element of continuity already there (or the message would be unintelligible). This continuity becomes the dominant *mode* of subsequent encounters. For faith that has made its fundamental option receives the word as nourishment, support, growth, in short as "upbuilding, encouragement, and consolation" (1 Cor 14:3) and not as the hammer shattering rock (Jer 23:29). There is continuity. There is familiarity. And while familiarity may run the risk of immunizing the hearer or the reader against surprise, if it proceeds from a genuine affective base, it may just as well alert him with even greater sensitivity to the ever new depths of understanding available in the text. To hear the word in this sense is no longer to leave one's land and one's father's home, but it is genuinely to come home. This at least seems to be the Pauline notion of *epignosis* and the role of the Paraclete in John.

The Hermeneutical Function of Community. In this connection I do not find much written on the hermeneutical function of the living community in which the word is read or heard. There is much written about how our culture and our experience condition our pre-understanding, but this is almost always assumed to be in dialectical opposition or resistance to the word that comes through preaching or text. There is not much written about the community that the word-event creates and how that community affects the interpretation of the word. Lonergan touches on this point when he writes:

> The classics ground a tradition. They create the milieu in which they are studied and interpreted. They produce in the reader through the cultural tradition, the mentality, the

Vorverständnis, from which they will be read, studied, interpreted.[28]

In the case of the scriptures, the tradition and the culture they create is often a counter-culture to the environment, a counter-culture which tests out the validity of the word for life, against the unquestioned assumptions of the prevailing culture. Such a tradition can, of course, be authentic or inauthentic, as Lonergan hastens to add, and it must always be open to challenge to greater authenticity both by the word and by the world. Nevertheless, such a tradition and community can be a precious interpretative assistance. It is not surprising that the word should sound strange to the point of incredibility if the hearer or reader cannot see its promises enfleshed in the context of human experience and relationships. On the other hand, the experience of community often alerts the interpreter to possibilities of meaning in the text which the individual deprived of that experience would never have suspected. One may be permitted to wonder if it is ever wise to attempt to interpret the scriptures in terms of a contemporary philosophy if one does not concomitantly explore what they mean to living communities that are finding life in them.

Unfortunately, the model of communication of the word that is operative in a great deal of the literature about the word-event is, when oral, that of the preacher in the pulpit communicating the pure word as a now-event to modern man. It is unrelated to a tradition and unrelated to an assembly as such, which might provide some assistance in the hermeneutical task. This lack of attention to the community's role in the process is not surprising, given the heavy influence on contemporary hermeneutical theory of existentialism, with its almost exclusive preoccupation with the individual.

One of the advantages of Ricoeur's linguistic paradigm is precisely that it stresses, over and against the total autonomy of the individual author, the common nature of language and the writer's entrance into that common human and community code of communication. At the reader's end of the spectrum, language is also a community matter, with objective meanings providing controls against arbitrariness or self-projection in the text. To the objection of subjectivism Ricoeur responds:

> This objection may be removed if we keep in mind that what is "made one's own" is not something mental, not the intention of another subject, presumably hidden behind the text, but the project of a world, the pro-position of a mode of being in the world that the text opens up in front of itself by means of its non-ostensive references. Far from saying that a subject already mastering his own way of being in the world projects the *a priori* of his self-understanding on the text and reads it into the text, I say that interpretation is the process by which disclosure of new modes of being—or if you prefer Wittgenstein to Heidegger, of new forms of life—gives to the subject a new capacity for knowing himself. If the reference of the text is the project of a world, then it is not the reader who primarily projects himself. The reader rather is enlarged in his capacity of self-projection by receiving a new mode of being from the text itself.

> Appropriation, in this way, ceases to appear as a kind of possession, as a way of taking hold of things; instead it implies a moment of dispossession of the egoistic and narcissistic ego. This process of dispossessing is the work of the kind of universality and atemporality emphasized in explanatory procedures. And this universality in its turn is linked to the disclosing power of the text as distinct from any kind of ostensive reference. Only the interpretation that complies with the injunction of the text, that follows the "arrow" of the sense and that tries to think accordingly, initiates a new self-understanding. In this self-understanding, I would oppose the self, which proceeds from the understanding of the text, to the ego, which claims to precede it. It is the text, with its universal power of world disclosure, which gives a self to the ego.[29]

But my question to this text of Ricoeur's is: What assurance do I have that my being changed by the text is a change for the better? Is it not equally possible that a text might change me for the worse, might move me not from ego to self but from self to ego, not to mention id or super-ego? Even a biblical text might do this if, for example, I am inspired by Mark 16:18 to glorify God by playing with rattlesnakes or drinking cyanide (who can say that such is not the "arrow" of the text?) — or, on the contrary, am moved by the eschatological expectation of the Sermon on the Mount to tighten around my neck the reins of a neo-legalism.

In other words, we are concerned with discernment, or with what Lonergan would call the judgment phase of cognition. And here I would submit that the truth of this judgment is greatly facilitated when it is done in a community that is striving to live the Gospel. It is in this environment that one finds a corrective and a supportive matrix for hearing or reading the word. One's chances of discovering the meaning of the word that came out of a similar community experience and of uncovering its meaningful and life-transforming power here and now are greatly enhanced. Granted that the judgment of the community can be wrong and granted that one cannot sell out one's personal judgment any more than one can sell one's conscience or soul, is this a greater risk than the risk of solipsism which the isolated individual runs even when he has available some objective linguistic controls?

Finally, perhaps it is not out of place to observe that the Judaeo-Christian community has always professed not only to be shaped by the word but also to be a people who *celebrate* the word. In fact, celebration of the word in the Old Testament and in the New appears to be the primary context in which the past event and the traditional word are interpreted. Authentic demythologizing is not a matter of philosophy but of cult. The word is understood when it is celebrated.

The Hermeneutical Function of Praxis. There is need for a further corrective. The word is, according to Jas 1:22-25 and other passages, understood only when it is lived:

Be doers of the word and not hearers only, deceiving your- selves. For if anyone is a hearer of the word and not a doer, he is like a man who observes his natural face in a mirror; for he observes himself and goes away and at once forgets what he was like. But he who looks into the perfect law, the law of liberty, and perseveres, being no hearer that forgets but a doer that acts, he shall be blessed in his doing.

This same point is made in the conclusion of the Sermon on the Mount (Mt 7:24-27; Lk 6:46-49).[30] There is a sense in which the word is like a practical hypothesis. To find whether the hypothesis is true, one must try it. Efforts to live it will have an important rebound on the interpretative task.

If the last two points sound too "Catholic," let me share with you my surprise upon reading the following from the pen of a Protestant scholar, David Lochhead:

We have a "problem" of private interpretation because we see hermeneutics as a primarily individualistic activity. Under the impact of the dominant liberal ideology of Western society, the insistence of the reformers on the freedom of conscience of the interpreter has led to a view of hermeneutics in which an interpretation is a matter of opinion of the individual and in which one opinion is as good as another.

Against this we need to insist that interpretation is not a matter of "opinion" but of *praxis*. Interpretation does not end when we draw the "moral" of a text, but when we act upon it. Secondly, the *praxis* which is the end of interpretation is not individual but corporate. In the last analysis, it is the involvement of the interpreter in a community of interpretation, in a community of *praxis*, which makes interpretation a meaningful activity.[31]

A Teaching Paradigm

We can now begin to bring our discussion to bear on our original question concerning a paradigm for teaching. I will say something first about Wink's paradigm before proposing mine.

Wink's Paradigm

For Wink the process of biblical study involves three dynamic moments. First, there is the moment of *fusion*. In the beginning of our study of the Bible we are already in a world of which the Bible is a part, and we are already predisposed to certain interpretations. By research, study, questioning, doubt, suspicion, and historical criticism, we are led to a negation of this fusion. And this leads to the second moment, *distance*. The problem with the method of historical criticism, says Wink, is that it stopped there. It is necessary to follow the critical method to its end, which is not linear but dialectical, where criticism rounds upon the critic, where reconstruction can happen only with the destruction of the destroyer, or where there is what Ricoeur calls "an archaeology of the subject".[32] This can happen, says Wink, through a psycho-analytical approach in which the psycho-social and symbolic meaning of the text illumines self-understanding and enables the closing of the circle in *communion*, the final step.

While I find these three steps valid, I believe the process is really more complex. And I am not persuaded that psycho-analytical and Jungian categories and the "sociology of knowledge" approach are a sufficiently comprehensive answer to the question. My own paradigm is complex and tentative, but I believe it incorporates the essential elements of a total hermeneutical and pedagogical process.

A Proposed Paradigm

1. *Awareness of my own world, experience and interest.* This awareness comes about not automatically but only in dialectic and in journey: in dialectic, inasmuch as I become aware of my world, the horizons and traditions in which I stand, as it is differentiated from others; in journey, inasmuch as I have a personal and collective history that has left its stamp upon me, a journey which is far from ended. Since I am more inclined to believe my history than to subject it to universal methodological doubt, it is better to stand on the journey past, with confession

both of its achievements and its limitations, and to be open to new turns and new vistas.

No one turns to a text unless one has a reason to do so — an experience or a question for which he hopes the text will provide illumination. If this procedure runs the risk of finding in the text only those things permitted by the question, it can equally be said that a new experience and a new question may lead us to discover elements and relationships in a text which old questions never saw. This is the point of departure in a hermeneutical paradigm offered by Juan-Luis Segundo:

> Firstly, there is our way of experiencing reality, which leads us to ideological suspicion. Secondly, there is the application of our ideological suspicion to the whole ideological super-structure in general and to theology in particular. Thirdly, there comes a new way of experiencing theological reality that leads us to exegetical suspicion, that is, to the suspicion that the prevailing interpretation of the Bible has not taken important pieces of data into account. Fourthly, we have our new hermeneutic, that is, our new way of interpreting the fountainhead of our faith (i.e., scripture) with the new elements at our disposal.[33]

One must, I think, accept Segundo's fourth point only with caution, lest one fall into total *eisegeses*, but the first three steps seem eminently valid, inasmuch as it is the real questions of our on-going experience that direct us to the text. The process is legitimate as long as we are aware that our experiences and our questions are not necessarily the ones that were in the mind of the author and that the text may give only a general answer or none at all to our question.

In the concrete teaching situation, the selection of a topic for a paper may be dictated precisely by the student's interest, which in turn emerges from his experience. If it is a question of approaching the study of a Gospel, for example, it is good that the student be able to formulate, however vaguely, his presuppositions as he approaches the text and the experiences which inspire his interest in this particular text.

Personal faith in the text as the word of God is often what occasions the inquiry. Such an initial stance certainly need not be less "scientific" than that of the scholar who approaches the text with faith in the adequacy of historical positivism. There is no *quaerens intellectum* without some kind of *fides*. In any case, what is needed at this stage is a surrender of the egoistic passion of prior control of the text, whether this surrender be expressed in the believer's prayer for enlightenment or in a less explicit "openness to transcendence," to use Stuhlmacher's term.[34]

2. *A simple reading of the text itself* noting areas of continuity and discontinuity with one's prior understandings. This will lead to questions.

3. *A literary analysis* of the text to see what is happening there. For example, one finds, in the story of Zacchaeus, that while Zacchaeus wanted to see Jesus, the surprise is that Jesus sees him. Here the method of structural analysis may be helpful in coming to terms as much as possible with what the text is saying.

4. *Amplification of the literary study* by historical-, form-, redaction-criticism, the occasion, and the author's intention and view as indicated from data outside the immediate text.

5. *Study of the history of function of the text.* If the student professes to belong to a community for which this text has been a life-giving one, consultation of its function in the transformation of that community is important. This step can be both critical of the tradition and of the student's understanding of the text. If the student, beyond mere academic interest, is also preparing to minister to that community, this step is vital. But if the text has, as Ricoeur insists, left the intentionality of the author and entered the space of human understanding available through language, the way it has spoken to succeeding generations is also significant to understanding the text itself, even apart from utilitarian interests.

6. *Understanding.* One begins to see the elements of the study fitting together. For the moment, the original questions of the student have receded before the immediate concern of the text. As the study continues, an important possibility is in prepara-

tion. The student's interest may begin to pass from his own original horizon into the horizon of the author. One becomes more interested, for the moment at least, in the question of the author and the text than in one's own. This is an important moment of trans-subjectivity.[35] It prepares the next step.

7. *Judgment.* In the light of his trans-subjective encounter with the text, the subject now makes a judgment. It is not only a judgment of the meaning of the text and of his understanding of it. It is, more importantly, the judgment the text is perceived to bear upon the subject's own world and experience which first inspired the question.

8. *Decision: conversion or deepening.* At this point the freedom of the subject must be defended against pan-objectivism, in which the individual is overwhelmed by the message of the text and surrenders to it out of some compulsive necessity. We are here at the delicate shrine of human freedom where it is best to take off our shoes. Christians will speak of grace or of the movement of the Holy Spirit — a movement that comes not merely from the sense of the compelling truth of the text but from the inner identification of the subject with it. This identification may be the "Amen" of the convert whose life is radically changed or a subsequent "Amen" of the believer who finds himself completed, fed, challenged, or fulfilled by the new insight.

This stage of the paradigm obviously goes beyond the mere external analysis, which seems to be the scope of most classroom situations. To share at this level is to belong to a faith community. It is to apply the text to a contemporary situation. However much such a step goes beyond the comfortable pale of the self-styled "objective" teacher, it is called for by a number of hermeneutical theorists, for whom there is no interpretation without application.[36]

9. *Dialectic: sharing, interaction.* At every one of the preceding steps it is important that there be interaction with other students, professors, members of one's own community, and members of other communities and traditions. However, if circumstances allow it, such an interaction would be particularly appropriate at this point among those who have experi-

enced a common summons by the text. This step could involve the comparison and classification of interpretations that different students have made of the text. A frank exchange then could follow on the various horizons of the students. Are the differences merely ones of perspective? Do they differ merely under the limitations of the canons of the different kinds of critical-interpretative tasks? Do they show up commitments to one's tradition that have not been questioned? Might they reveal the presence or absence of intellectual, moral, or religious conversion?

This kind of sharing of insights and values can be an excellent preparation for the next step.

10. *Celebration*. This step departs even more from the normal classroom situation. Celebration and ritual have been man's perennial way of finding meaning. For such celebrations the traditional texts are important but ancillary. Most of the biblical texts, as most religious texts in general, were created in one way or another as scripts for celebration, and thus there is a surplus of meaning which the text, like the tip of the iceberg, only suggests and which can be revealed only when relived in ritual. In this context the text is interpreted by anagogical exposition and then dramatized in a way in which the entire community acts out the meaning ritually. For millions of Christians in pre-literate ages and cultures it was this, along with the preached word, and not the study of a text, which completed the hermeneutical circle.

11. *Doing*. Finally, since the biblical text most often has to do with practical wisdom, its truth cannot be experienced or verified merely academically. It must be tested by doing. Doing the text is as important a dimension for understanding as enacting is important to understand the text of a Shakespearean play. For most biblical texts, action is part of their very intentionality.

Conclusion

Needless to say, the steps outlined cannot be airtight compartments. As one passes through each of the steps, there is feedback gained on the validity of the others. The hermeneutical circle is thus really a spiral giving mounting comprehension of whole and parts.

As for the teaching of scripture, one may appropriately question how much of this process can be accomplished in the classroom. There are, after all, limitations of time, and there must be specialization if material is to be covered at any depth. However, I believe that if we have sinned in theological education, it has been of late more in the direction of specialization than of synthesis, of analysis than of understanding, of data than of meaning. And perhaps those who need most to learn the hermeneutical function of community are our faculties of theology themselves. The student often wanders from one classroom to another, to chapel and to hospital ward, carrying upon his own shoulders the burden of integrating what often the faculty of theology have shown little interest in getting together. Perhaps the detailing of a possible process of learning in scriptural studies will alert us to the role and limitations of our particular specialty within the framework of a larger holistic experience, in which alone the discovering of meaning can be brought to term. The student's cry for meaning need not be a cry for instant and effortless relevance. It may well be a cry to find the living God in what is professed to be his word.

SUMMARY AND CONCLUSION

James A. O'Brien

A symposium on "Scripture in the Charismatic Renewal" was called in response to the pastoral situation of people in the charismatic renewal. First of all, scripture has been central to the charismatic experience, to its growth and acceptance. God has demonstrated that the word contains power for preaching, teaching, and evangelizing. These uses of scripture are not unique to the charismatic renewal. However, our experience of the word has caused us to ask: What is God teaching us through the different uses of his word? How can these lessons be used for the total renewal of the Church? However, not every use of scripture is a proper use. In other words, certain pastoral concerns about particular practices have arisen in the charismatic renewal — most notably, the issue of fundamentalism. So we ask: How can we seek to alleviate some of the pastoral concerns associated with particular uses of scripture in the charismatic renewal?

The reflections shared in this section are the fruit of group interaction. After the presentation of the four preceding papers, biblical scholars, diocesan liaisons, theologians, and respected leaders reacted to the papers in light of their own experience. These remarks are an attempt to gather, distill, and present the thought, discussion, and pastoral recommendations of all the conference participants.

The Context

The relation of Bible and Church is a complex one. Avery Dulles brilliantly points out a number of key theological issues which contribute to the complexity of this relationship. Through a dialetical method, he presents the thought and argumentation surrounding the differences between the Protestant and Catholic approaches to the word; the formation of scriptures; the role of the Christian community; the criteria used for compiling the final scriptural canon; the importance of the Old Testament in revelation; the place of faith in approaching the Bible; the process of divine inspiration; the role of biblical scholarship in the Church; the importance of the *magisterium* in relation to the interpretation of the Bible; and the place of individual interpretation.

Though these complexities do exist and do have a significant impact upon the usage of scripture, the Bible is becoming increasingly prominent in the lives of more and more people. There is no question that we are in the midst of a "return to the Bible." Thus, in order to understand how scripture is being used in the charismatic renewal, it is necessary to reflect upon the context in which the charismatic renewal is developing. Just as a solitary northern pine on a wilderness hill derives its meaning and beauty from the totality of the landscape, so too the meaning of scripture usage in the charismatic renewal should be viewed against the broad background of Church and ecumenism. The context for the different usages of scripture can be summarized in five overarching areas: affirmation of God's action; renewal in the church; interpretation of scripture; ecumenical influence; and leadership formation.

The Affirmation of God's Action

Our starting point must be the affirmation of God's presence, action, and power among his people. The Lord reveals himself when his people prayerfully reflect, and proclaim the word. The Letter to the Hebrews sums up this revelatory character of scripture by saying, "Indeed, God's word is living and effective, sharper than any two-edged sword. It penetrates and divides soul and spirit, joints and marrow; it judges the reflections and thoughts of the heart" (Heb 4:12). Again, in the Gospel of John, the Samaritan townsfolk testify that they believe in Jesus as Savior not only on the testimony of the woman at the well but rather on the basis that they have heard (believed) the words of Jesus. Christians today continue to encounter the God revealed in the living word.

In the charismatic renewal, men and women are announcing the basic Gospel message, and, in prayer meetings and seminars, are delivering teachings based on biblical themes and images. The scriptural word is proclaimed in communal gatherings, prayer with others, witnessing, and bringing people to Christ. Individual believers frequently pray and read the scriptures daily, sometimes opening the Bible spontaneously under the guidance of the Spirit, and other times following a particular book or thematic development of the Bible. Scripture, whether preached, taught, or proclaimed to the assembly, is complimentary to the prophetic word. Through prophecy the Lord continues to speak, guide, and direct the community. Prophecy is another means of tapping God's word to us. However, the authenticity of the prophetic word must be judged by its fidelity to and affinity with the scriptural word.

Most assuredly, charismatics have a strong sense of God speaking to them through the scriptures. The word is a power that prompts repentance, holds out the hope of healing; challenges Christ's followers to embrace the cross and serve the poor; and invites all into even deeper union with God. Saint Paul says, "I am not ashamed of the Gospel. It is the power of God leading everyone who believes in it to salvation" (Rom 1:16).

The spontaneous opening of the Bible for guidance has always been a part of our tradition. For example, St. Francis of Assisi prayed in this fashion. Sometimes this practice is referred to as "cracking the Bible" or "Bible roulette." Certainly this practice may be abused. A story is told about a person who asked the Lord for a word and opened to the hanging of Judas. He was confused and asked the Lord to clarify the meaning of the text. Then he opened to "Go and do likewise." Obviously the spontaneous opening of the Bible cannot be our sole principle of discernment nor our only means for making decisions. It is simply one way of asking the Lord to speak through his word.

In sum, dialogue between the theologians and the people of God must ensue. The people are saying quite clearly that they are experiencing the presence and power of God in and through prayer, preaching, teaching, witnessing, evangelizing, and charismatic word gifts. Their lives are being changed, and their hearts are being touched. Likewise, they are vocal about the fact that not every form of biblical teaching and preaching edifies, builds up, and touches the interior person. They are, I believe, speaking the word of the Lord to those of us formally involved in the ministries of preaching, teaching, and theologizing. However, at the same time, theologians are "people of God" and mediate God's word to us as experienced by the total Christian community. The charism of scholarship must always inform the preaching, teaching, and interpretation of scripture in light of the tradition of the Church. A dialogue among all God's people — whether they be theologians, ministers, single people, truck drivers, or nuclear physicists — is essential to our ability to grow in fidelity to God's living word.

Renewal in the Church

The usage of scripture in the charismatic renewal must be seen in light of the entire renewal of the Church.

Since Vatican Council II, the Church has undergone considerable religious change. In some fifteen years since the Council, the liturgy has been celebrated in the vernacular; worship, song, and community have been emphasized in the Eucharist; healing has been given new emphasis in penance and the anointing of the sick; ministry is shared in our parishes among priests, sisters, lectors, eucharistic ministers, parish councils, and others; and worshipers are encouraged to receive communion in the hand and to partake of the eucharistic cup. The quality of religious change and *aggiornamento* has depended to a great extent upon the type of local leadership, preparation, and ongoing education available.

Both the positive uses of scripture and those that have generated a certain amount of pastoral concern are not unique to the charismatic renewal. They are also reflected in the general Catholic population. The desire for scripture teaching and the frequent misuse of scripture must be seen amid the wider milieu of the whole Church. Despite recent liturgical, spiritual, and ministerial developments, scripture appears to be the one area where most people remain unformed. The majority of Catholics, not just those in prayer meetings, approach the scriptures literally.

Recently, a suburban parish in New Jersey invited a prominent biblical scholar to participate in an adult education series explaining recent developments in the infancy narratives. Midway through the initial presentation, quite a few people began leaving. The people who left complained that the scholar was destroying the Christmas stories. The point, I believe, is that the Bible must become *the book of the people*, not just *the book of the scholars*. It's important that great pastoral sensitivity be exercised then the insights of biblical criticism are shared.

The majority of people who belong to our prayer communities have their primary religious identity in the local parish. The parish community celebrates the major events of life — birth, adulthood, sickness, marriage, and death — and has responsibility for the formation of the total community. Fundamentalism is not only a concern of the charismatic renewal; it is a matter of some importance for the entire Church. Like prayer groups, our parishes are eager to tap the tremendous power of God's word and to deal with inappropriate uses of scripture. The Church faces the tremendous hunger of God's people for the living word, and the need to provide biblical teaching which both informs and inspires.

The Interpretation of Scripture

In our discussions we found that it was helpful to distinguish between the usage of scripture and the interpretation of scripture. For example, a particular biblical text can often be used to enlighten or even enhance a given theme or reflection. Homiletics frequently uses this teaching technique. However, whenever a speaker indicates that an interpretation is *the meaning* of the text, this judgment must be informed by the charism of scholarship. A pastoral problem occurs when the spiritual sense — what God said to the individual preaching or teaching — is presented to the group as the meaning of the text, or as the only meaning possible.

During the group discussion Avery Dulles was very helpful in reformulating the three levels of meaning in scripture: (1) the *literal*—the meaning of the biblical text as intended by the evangelist writer; (2) the *dogmatic*—the meaning as revealed through the lived experience of the Christian community in history; and (3) the *spiritual*—the meaning which the Lord speaks to individuals when they meditate on the word. This last sense of scripture can be used to highlight a point in a teaching, give testimony to the Lord, or witness to those in need of evangelism. Charismatic Christians, especially those in teaching ministries, are encouraged to have an informed approach to scripture in order to appreciate the full revelation of God in Jesus Christ.

Ecumenical Influence

Increased contact and interaction with Christians of other denominations has most definitely opened Catholics to a new familiarity with the Bible. The Protestant traditions and assemblies place a priority on God's presence and power in the word. By means of these ecumenical contacts. Catholics have learned much about the baptism in the Spirit, the gifts of the Spirit, the ministry of deliverance, techniques for evangelism, and the importance of a personal decision in accepting Jesus as the Lord of one's life. Happily, the exchange is mutual, and Catholics are sharing the treasures of their tradition too: critical biblical scholarship, the Eucharist and sacraments, the importance of community and authority, contemplation, and an appreciation for great women and men throughout history.

The charismatic renewal among all the churches is pointing out that God's word in scripture may well be the common ground, the meeting place for authentic ecumenism. The whole charismatic movement is "scripture conscious." Scripture may well be the point of convergence, where Christians share their gifts and honestly face their differences.

With the notable exception of the Sunday homily, Catholics have been slow to form their people biblically. Hence, many people in prayer groups are being formed in their approach to the Bible by other Christian faiths. The literature sold at book tables, tapes available from denominational and nondenominational sources, Bible studies, the multitude of radio broadcasts, and T.V. ministries, such as Oral Roberts or the 700 Club, are forming people's approach to scripture. Where this exposure had led to a literal approach to reading the Bible, pastoral problems have arisen. Some people have left the Church in order to "be fed."

These pastoral observations are offered not to discourage Christians from sharing the scriptures with one another, but to point to the need to provide more Bible teaching in response to the tremendous hunger for God's word. In this way, an environment for authentic ecumenical interaction can be created, where Christians remain faithful to their own tradition while sharing the riches of other Christian churches.

Leadership Formation

Prayer group leaders are key to the future growth and development of the charismatic renewal and its integration into the full life of the Church. The diocesan liaisons as well as the American Bishops and the National Service Committee recognize the necessity of forming leaders. Leadership formation consists of something other than training competent theologians. Professional skills will not suffice. Rather, adequate leadership formation involves several factors: the personal spiritual development of the leader; adequate skills for ministry (which do involve being theologically informed) and a community where God's word is lived. Furthermore, since Christian ministry is shared or corporate, it is recommended that the entire pastoral team, or all those in the teaching ministry, be formed and inspired together, rather than simply functioning as isolated individuals with certain responsibilities in the prayer group.

Put more practically, the issue before us is: How can prayer group leaders be formed and informed so that they can teach in the prayer community with competence? Many communities are blessed with individuals who have professional training in theology — priests, sisters, brothers, deacons, and lay women and men with degrees in religious education, for example. Guest speakers, workshops, retreats, days of renewal, and regional and national conferences also assist in the spiritual formation of people. Nevertheless, leaders should be formed both individually and corporately, with the proper skills to do "Bible teaching." They needn't become scholars, but they should have an informed approach to scripture. Each state, diocese, and city must work out the practical details of how this formation should take place. People are hungering for scripture teaching. We need to beg the Lord Jesus to multiply the loaves and the fishes of his word once again.

Therefore, the use of scripture in the charismatic renewal must first of all be seen in context. The context consists of these factors: (1) prayerful people are experiencing the presence and power of God in his word; (2) biblical renewal in the whole Church is the backdrop for the usage of scripture in the charismatic renewal; (3) the charism of scholarship needs to inform the interpretation of the word if that interpretation is to remain faithful to the community of the Church; (4) authentic ecumenism opens the word to many Catholics and offers an opportunity to share the Lord and his word; and (5) the future of the charismatic renewal rests upon the spiritual formation of its leaders and their integration within the Church. Now let us turn to the specific uses of scripture.

Particular Uses of Scripture

In one of his letters St. Paul presents some helpful insights for our usage of scripture. He says, "All scripture is inspired of God and is useful for teaching, for reproof, correction, and training in holiness so that the person of God may be fully competent and equipped for every good work" (2 Tm 3:16). Paul reminds us that scripture is the word of God, that its origin is divine inspiration. Certainly this Pauline proclamation does not undermine the humanness of the word of God. Richard Rohr reminds us of the human dimension of scripture when he says, "The people created the Book. The Book did not create the people."[1] In reality scripture is the word of God in human words. The word, like the incarnate Jesus, is both human and divine. Furthermore, Paul informs us that scripture not only prepares but actually empowers a person for service to others. One who reads, prays, and indeed lives the word of God is "equipped for every good work." Scripture may be used for teaching, direction, and growth in holiness.

Teaching

Most local prayer groups, especially the smaller ones, are facing the task of providing more adequate teaching for the ongoing growth of the group.[2] Put simply, many people soon ask "After the *Life in the Spirit Seminars*, then what?" The first form of teaching which one usually encounters upon beginning to attend prayer meetings is evangelistic in its thrust. The majority of prayer groups implement either *The Life in the Spirit Seminars, You Will Receive Power,* or *Friendship With the Lord*.[3] All three are designed to bring people to deeper faith and to initiate new members into the charismatic renewal. Books, tapes, and conferences also assist in forming teachers and supplying content for teachings. With renewed interest in scripture there has arisen a specific demand for what might best be called "scripture teaching." Inevitably the question surfaces, "Who in our prayer group is qualified to do scripture teaching?"

Participants in this symposium found it helpful to distinguish between various types of teaching which made use of scripture. Teaching may be apologetical, inspirational, or catechetical — to name just three types. For example, particular Pauline texts from the First Letter to the Corinthians, chapters 12-14, were often used in the early 1970's to justify and authenticate the exercise of the charisms among prayer group members. This use of scripture served more to illustrate a point of teaching rather than to act as a textual analysis of Paul's experience of charism. Therefore, an important distinction was made between "teaching with scripture" and "teaching scripture." "Teaching with scripture" is viewed as a general teaching drawing upon relevant passages from the Old and New Testaments, whereas "teaching scripture" is specifically concerned with the interpretation of the text through certain exegetical skills. Both are present and needed in the charismatic renewal.

105

As the discursion developed, "Bible teaching" as a particular genre of teaching fast became the focus of attention. Many Protestant preachers and evangelists enjoy great success doing Bible teaching. What then makes this form of teaching so attractive and what are its characteristics? Bible teaching is not just any type of scripture teaching. According to Gabe Meyer from Los Angeles, Bible teaching is *personal, practical,* and *inspirational.* George Martin further commented that Bible teaching provides a practical exposition of a text from scripture, interprets its meaning, and applies it to the lives of the listeners. It encourages the Bible study leader and the group participants to witness and share how the particular biblical text applies in one's own life. Thus, Bible teaching as a genre certainly highlights the spiritual sense of the word.

Bible studies are in great demand. People are attending Bible studies wherever they are offered. Since there is a relative lack of Bible teaching among Catholics, many are attending Bible studies and home Bible groups associated with nondenominational or Pentecostal churches. Some of these Catholics point out that their parishes do not provide Bible teaching or that the teaching provided is "too scholarly, or too dry" and does not address their personal lives. Until this situation can be remedied, priests and prayer group leaders are encouraged to be in good relationships with those who lead these local Bible studies in order to avoid any ecumenical difficulties.

A further consideration in regard to Bible teaching is the formation of competent teachers. How are Bible teachers formed? From some well-known preachers and evangelists we learn that academic courses in seminary or university alone are not adequate preparation for this style of teaching. In other words, exegesis, form-criticism and teaching techniques are not sufficient in themselves. Rather Bible teaching presupposes one's spiritual formation and is frequently learned from a gifted Bible teacher. The relationship between student and master is one of "discipleship." Much more is shared than mere skills. Therefore, among Catholics there is a need for environments of prayer and study, where men and women can be formed as Bible teachers. Adequate Bible teaching is not only exegetically and dogmatically informed; it also communicates itself existentially. Certainly our seminaries and universities hold out great hope in forming Bible teachers, but at the same time, educational and spiritually formative experiences must be made available to women and men, married and single, who have been given gifts by God to proclaim his word. Men and women in religious orders should not be the only ones availing themselves of this formation.

George Montague's paradigm for teaching scripture is insightful and most definitely encompassing. He quite rightly stresses the necessary theological skills, the importance of living and integrating the word into one's life, the necessity of living the word in community through interaction and celebration, and the resulting service which emanates from internalizing the word, both individually and collectively. Without questioning the scope of the paradigm,[4] one could ask how many people presently teaching in prayer meetings (or in pulpits!) have the theological sophistication to carry out steps 3, 4, and 5 of his paradigm: structural analysis, form criticism, and the historical usage of the text? It seems that a simplified model containing the thrust of the proposed paradigm would be most helpful to people.

In summary, four pastoral needs were acknowledged:

1. There is need in the Catholic Church for Bible teaching — teaching which has the characteristics of being doctrinally and exegetically informed as well as being personal, practical, and inspirational.

2. There is need for formative experiences, both on a professional and informal level, where men and women can be trained as Bible teachers. Two such programs are now in existence: the College of Steubenville in Steubenville, Ohio, sponsors a Bible Institute and St. Mary's University in San Antonio, Texas, sponsors the Catholic Charismatic Bible Institute.

3. There is immediate need to teach scripture in response to the tremendous hunger for God's word. This teaching, whether "teaching with scripture" or "teaching

scripture," should be theolog; a ly sound and applicable to daily living.

4. There is need for more courses, tapes, literature, and workshops on scripture teaching, especially for leaders and those teaching in prayer meetings. Prayer groups are encouraged to make use of those among them who have formal training in theology as well as others in their local diocese with this kind of background. *Reading Scripture as the Word of God* by George Martin was specifically endorsed by the symposium participants.

The Directive Use of Scripture

The precise sense in which scripture is normative for Christian faith and the development of doctrine in the Church is still very much debated among theologians. Scripture certainly holds a place of great importance because it puts us in touch with the words and deeds of Jesus and the words about Jesus as recorded by the early Christians. Scripture can be said to be generally directive for all Christians.[5] The Bible reveals God and his love, cuts into our hearts, changes our direction, convicts us of wrongdoing, calls us to repentance, and offers guidance and direction for our lives. Since the scriptural word assists us in our personal surrender to Jesus as Lord and aids us as we journey in faith, scripture can be said to be directive, to offer guidance.

However, in light of developments in the charismatic renewal, a more precise question can be asked: Are the scriptures meant to give us specific answers to questions and situations that are current or personal to us? If they are, then the exercise of personal discernment with regard to the biblical text becomes very important.

A few examples may help to clarify this point. Frank MacNutt in his book entitled *Healing* indicates that God generally desires his people to experience healing rather than to be bound by the crippling effects of suffering and sickness. Whether the Lord is healing *this* woman of cancer when she appears to be in the last stages of her life is a specific judgment of discernment confirmed by medical science. We all know of situations where someone while praying with another person asked for a passage, opened to a "healing text," and proclaimed the sick person healed. The damage which comes from misuse of the biblical text and lack of discernment can sometimes be irreparable.

Another example illustrates how a particular text did help a woman in her search for guidance. In a neighboring parish a woman was praying whether she should ask a certain priest to be her spiritual director. She hesitated to ask him because she wasn't sure that he would be right for her. After she asked the Lord to speak to her, she opened to the Second Book of Kings and read about Elijah killing all the messengers sent by the King (2 Kgs 1:9-18). She wondered whether asking this priest to be her spiritual director might have the same impact upon her spiritual life. Then her eyes fell upon verse 15, "The angel of the Lord said to Elijah, 'Go down with him; you need not be afraid of him.' " She believed that was her answer. The relationship has been a great blessing to both of them over the years.

What are some of the pastoral issues related to the directive use of scripture? First of all, when one is using scripture in this fashion, one must face "the hermeneutical gap," i.e., the gap between what the text meant when the author was writing and what the text means today. In other words, the meaning cannot always be equated with the literal word. A cultural disparity exists between the twentieth-century reader and the first-century Jewish Christians. To ignore the difference in culture and language is to have a historical approach to the scriptures. Such a gulf between then and now can only be bridged by a hermeneutic of some sort. Every hermeneutic must be informed by personal faith lest the word be robbed of its power.

Second, there can be no doubt that people are experiencing guidance through prayerful reflection upon the word. What is most laudable in this devotional practice of asking the Lord for a passage is the desire to be judged by the word of God and the desire to seek the Lord for an answer to a particular question or situation in one's life. Jesus himself says, "Doing the will of him who sent me and bringing his work to completion is my food" (Jn 4:34). Though asking the Lord for a passage can never be the sole principle of discernment, a legitimate use of scripture in prayer is the directive use.

Third, there are some difficulties associated with this devotional practice. It is a distortion of the sacred writings to make of them a collection of answers to all life's possible situations. As one pastor said, "Some people have simply replaced the Baltimore Catechism with the Bible, swapped one set of rules for another." Lurking behind this "black and white" approach to the scriptures is, of course, the belief in *sola scriptura* and a literalist reading of individual texts. This approach is always inadequate.

The terms "Bible cracking" or "Bible roulette" can refer to a simplistic seeking of God's word. At worst, this may degenerate into a magical approach to the scriptures. One simply turns on the electric switch, and God's word appears instantly as light. The Lord is not accessible in this fashion. He reveals himself in faith over a period of time. Discernment involves a process of continual seeking and its accompanying confirmations.

There is often a specialized language which sometimes goes along with the directive use of scripture. Such jargon is usually ambiguous. "Standing on the word," "standing under the word," "the Lord says" are examples of such terminology. Some people have indeed been victimized by jargon. When these expressions are used as a reminder of the promises of Jesus and the depth of word they are laudable. However, when they absolutize the Word of God apart from the context of the living tradition of the Church, they tend to reinforce fundamentalism.

In sum, I would say that the crux of the directive use of scripture consists in discerning the action of the Spirit in a particular situation. Reverend William O'Brien, from the Community of God's Love in Rutherford, New Jersey, put it very well when he said, "It seems that a better way of understanding the experience of praying for directive passages from scripture is to see them as confirming or denying what is already going on in the heart of the person. Such an understanding of the experience does not divorce the text from its original context." This sense of the scripture being used by the Lord to identify his action within a person's heart is developed most admirably by Paul

Hinnebusch in his paper "Using the Scriptures In Prayer."

Prayer and Sanctification

St. Paul reminds his readers of the depth of holiness to which they are called when he says, "God chose us in him before the world began, to be holy and blameless in his sight, to be full of love" (Eph 1:4). Scripture forms Christ's followers in prayer and the ongoing growth in holiness.[6] Particular books of the Bible can be more useful than others to help individuals confront different life situations. With this in mind, the symposium participants thought it useful to call attention to *specific biblical themes* that might nourish the prayer of contemporary Christians.

Old Testament. The Old Testament is a rich source of religious images capable of nurturing prayer and growth in holiness. Although the fullness of revelation comes in the person of Jesus, nonetheless, the Old Testament contains the record of God's revelation of himself in history and the response of the Hebrew People to this revelation. Such biblical images in the Old Testament are *symbolic* and *revelatory* — they mediate the presence of God and allow man to meet the God who reveals.

The creation accounts affirm the essential goodness of the world God has made. The fundamental goodness of creation and the world should never be obscured by the rhetoric and images that shape apocalyptic literature, particularly when that rhetoric is distorted by the excesses of contemporary prophets of doom. Authentic Christian hope never denies the goodness of God's creation.

Hebrew covenant theology summons every generation of believers to constant fidelity and obedience to God and his word. The Exodus calls the believer to freedom from oppression and to freedom in commitment to God and others. The story of Exodus recalls the fact that even today God's people are a pilgrim people, always on the move toward God. It warns God's chosen that committed faith leads individuals and communities into the desert of testing, trial, and longing for God, of repentance and trust. "So I will allure her; I will lead her into the desert and speak to her heart" (Hos 2:16).

The psalms are a perennially rich source for Christian prayer. They reflect a sense of God's presence in all creation, the need for heartfelt and interior repentance, the great anguish of the soul while searching for the Lord in trial, and tremendous worship and praise of the faithful God who saves. It's little wonder that the psalms have been adopted as the rightful prayer of the Church.

The prophetic books of the Bible mirror the struggle for individual and corporate growth in holiness. Hosea, Isaiah, Jeremiah, Ezekiel, to name a few, reveal their own personal odyssey in responding to the living word of the Lord. They also dramatically point to the God who always attempts to call a wayward people back to himself. The prophetic books teach us what it means to confront in God's name the social, economic, and political problems of our day. These works are particularly pertinent today as the charismatic renewal begins to take seriously God's call for justice in the world.

Both the Book of Job and the Songs of the Suffering Servant in Isaiah, chapters 49-53, force us to confront in faith the mystery of human suffering. Not everyone is healed. Every day people die of starvation. Nation wars against nation, cancer and heart disease silently prey upon good women and men, and people continue to be oppressed because of race, creed, economic position, and avarice. The evil that pervades the world remains a mystery. These prophetic books of the Bible share meaning where there would otherwise be darkness.

New Testament. For the believing Christian the New Testament offers the clearest insight into the meaning of growth in Christian holiness. It is Jesus who reveals the way to the Father and shows Christians how to live together in faith. To be holy is to be transformed by the Spirit in God's image.

Transformation in the Spirit makes specific demands on those who confess Jesus as Lord.[7] Jesus calls us to a trust and a faith in God, which like his own, is unconditional. Faith in the God who is Father, Son, and Spirit must be open-ended. It is God alone, not ourselves, who dictates the terms of relationship to him.

Faith in God must come to practical expression in worship,

both in personal prayer and in the shared worship of the Christian *koinonia*. The test of the authenticity of Christian worship is mutual forgiveness in the image of Jesus. That forgiveness must be sustained in the face of rejection and persecution. The suffering it demands must be accepted in advance.

Christian faith also demands a willingness to live not by bread alone but by every word that comes from God's mouth. By feeding the hungry, clothing the naked, and performing other such works of mercy, a Christian witnesses to personal faith in the coming reign of God. By the same token the Christian labors not in order to amass wealth but to avoid being burdensome to others and to have something to share with others in Jesus's name. Hospitality, especially to the needy and dispossessed, is then a fundamental expression of Christian faith. This sharing, born of faith in God, must proceed on the basis of need, not of merit. It excludes no one in principle and reaches across personal, economic, political, and social barriers.

It is Jesus who summons us to faith-sharing, to mutual love and forgiveness of one another in his image within the context of a community of faith and worship. Those who follow him in holiness must then live by values very different from those that shape much of contemporary society. And, like Jesus, his followers must stand prophetically opposed to those social and political structures which cannot be reconciled with the ideals of Christian conduct he inculcated. Like him, they must accept in advance the suffering which comes when they stand in opposition to human hypocricy, selfishness, injustice and oppression.

Finally, Christian sharing must extend beyond the sharing of material possessions. The sharing of faith, hope, and love, the sharing of the charisms of the Spirit, must also authenticate and give meaning to Christian worship.

Different books of the New Testament are able to address different needs in individuals and in prayer communities. The Gospel of Mark was written for a community suffering persecution. Jesus is the Messiah who is hidden but later revealed. He is the *suffering servant* by whose death we have salvation. This gospel proclamation will nourish the faith of those who are called upon to suffer in any way for Jesus' sake.

The Gospel of Matthew was written for a community fragmented in its leadership and membership. In this Gospel, Jesus is presented as the Messiah-King, the new Moses whose teachings become the source of life for Christians. Matthew's Gospel contains the most references to the Old Testament and frequently refers to the fulfillment of the Mosaic Law. Matthew invites any community faced with similar problems to focus their minds and hearts on Jesus, his example and teaching, so that he might draw them back into union in the obedience of faith and love.

The Gospel of Luke and the Acts of the Apostles will be of special help to individuals and communities who need to grow in their willingness to share their gifts and goods. Luke's Gospel is known as the Gospel of the Spirit, of prayer, joy, mercy, and the poor. Acts presents how the early Christians shared their lives together in community. These two works remind individuals and communities whose piety is tinged with elitism and narrow exclusivism that they must acknowledge in word and deed the universal scope of divine salvation and love.

The Epistles of John and the Gospel of John will nourish the faith and prayer-life of those who desire to deepen in contemplative openness to God. Jesus is the absolute center of John's Gospel. He is the preexistent, incarnate word who reveals the Father for those who believe. Nicodemus, the Samaritan woman, the man born blind — all represent the journey of the individual Christian to ever-deepening faith in Jesus. The Evangelist John records only one command — the command to love as Christ loved. Due to the symbolic nature of the writing, the Gospel of John invites deeper contemplation of the person of Jesus and highlights the sacramental dimension of Christian community.

The letters of Paul speak more explicitly than any other New Testament document of the relation between the charisms of the Spirit and growth in Christian holiness. Paul insists more explicitly than any other New Testament author that Christian sharing must proceed on an *institutional* as well as *individual* basis. Communities must be willing to come to the aid of other communities less fortunate than themselves.

Those involved in the charismatic renewal are encouraged to cultivate a variety of *legitimate prayer forms*. Each spirituality, whether Franciscan, Ignatian, or Dominican, emphasizes an aspect of the mystery of God. Each spirituality brings its own gift. Each Christian's spiritual life should have a natural balance – a balance of time spent alone, group prayer, sharing, Eucharist, scripture, and service. Likewise, group prayer needs to be supplemented by private meditation, the contemplation of the word, and the prayerful reading of doctrinal and devotional works.

Individuals will also experience a variety of *rhythms and needs* in their prayer life. For example, people who have been in the charismatic renewal for some time may experience their initial sense of intimacy with the Lord giving way to what seems like a real desert in their prayer-life. Or again, a person may be very expressive in worship during private prayer, and later this stance may shift to a quieter form of prayer – a time of simply "being with the Lord." Prayer communities also find that the Lord leads them through different phases, or rhythms. Diverse expressions, needs, and legitimate prayer forms should always be respected in the context of Christian communities.

Charismatic Christians should expect that they will experience, from time-to-time, periods of dryness within prayer. Fidelity to prayer during such periods of aridity is extremely important. It is itself a form of prayer and an expression of faith. It will help in such times of dryness to read the word of God even though little sensible consolation accompanies it. Charismatic Christians may even be led by God into an experience of what St. John of the Cross calls the "dark night of the soul." It is a period of purifying darkness in prayer, in which faith, hope, and love deepen and intensify in ways that are scarcely perceptible at the time.

Charismatic Christians ought to expect and desire a deepening in prayer that goes beyond mere exuberance. They are urged to look for the fruits of the Spirit in personal and shared prayer. The presence of the gifts and the fruits of the Spirit as well as the deepening of faith, hope, and love are the surest signs of progress in holiness.

Charismatic Christians are exhorted to use scripture for prayer in an informed and intelligent way. Both the study and meditation of God's word should be encouraged. Each diocese is exhorted to put at the disposal of its prayer groups its own resources of instruction so that charismatic prayer may be nourished by a sound understanding of scripture and Christian doctrine. Bible study, adult education, and the availability of reliable reading materials will all be of help in this regard.

Finally, charismatic Christians will find in the Bible a common religious language. The word of God can draw together married couples by giving them shared images, ideas, and beliefs that interpret their mutual love for one another in Christ. The Bible also offers a common language which unites the Christian churches. Active concern for the advancement of ecumenism and for the healing of the divisions that separate the churches is an important expression of contemporary growth in Christian holiness.

Concluding Remarks

This gathering of theologians, diocesan liaisons, and leaders to discuss the use of scripture in the charismatic renewal came out of the experience of reflecting upon and acting out ways to pastor prayer communities within various diocese. First of all, on the negative side, we were faced with fundamentalism and the pastoral consequences which emerge from a literal reading of the scriptures. More positively, we saw an ever-increasing hunger for scripture teaching among God's people. I personally came to Milwaukee looking for answers, strategies, and programs and left the symposium with questions, a clearer assessment of the complexity of issues surrounding the authentic use of scripture, and most importantly, a greater appreciation for the depth and beauty of the God who reveals himself in his word.

God's people are longing for adequate understanding and familiarity with the word, and for the ability to live out its implications in their own life and community. This situation is not merely a concern of charismatics; it is a Church concern as well.

Second, it was emphasized that scholarship need not be mistrusted. Among certain people in the charismatic renewal, scholarship has been viewed as a mere exercise of intellectualism, devoid of faith. This attitude has been termed "anti-intellectualism."

During one of the more humorous moments, someone addressed the mutual mistrust of scholar and lay person by citing the example of the bumblebee and the aeronautical engineer. The aeronautical engineer, as the story goes, says that, on paper and by design, the bumblebee cannot fly; its body is too plump and its wings too short; its weight is far too heavy to be lifted by such tiny wings. However, as we know by personal observation, the bumblebee flies — maybe not too straight or too far — but it flies! Some people's use of scripture may not always reflect the best theology, but they fly. They experience God.

The impact that this story had upon us was that we took seriously other people's and our own experience of God in the word. We acknowledged that historical-criticism when used alone corrodes faith, that not every form of scripture teaching builds faith. People in the charismatic renewal need not mistrust the theological insights of scholars. Scholarship is a charism. Like all other charisms, scholarship must be dynamically related to the other gifts of the Spirit and be firmly rooted in Christian community. Only through faith-filled dialogue between the professsional and non-professional can the light of the Lord be shed on the different uses of scripture.

Finally, the future of the charismatic renewal rests upon the development of prayer group leaders. The life of the prayer community is dependent upon good teaching, which for the most part is done by leaders before, during, and after the prayer meeting. The leadership's understanding and approach to scripture will have a great impact on the group's understanding and approach to scripture. Therefore, the pastoral task which lies ahead consists of guiding the spiritual formation of men and women who are competent with the word. At first glance this task may seem overwhelming. However, the Church has the resources; new institutes for Bible teaching among Catholics are emerging; new leaders will be called forth. Dioceses in particular will need to organize programs for leader formation. It is the Lord himself who is drawing us to his word.

The Lord said to me: Son of man, eat what is before you; eat this scroll, then go, speak to the house of Israel. So I opened my mouth and he gave me the scroll to eat. Son of man, he then said to me, feed your belly and fill your stomach with this scroll I am giving you. I ate it, and it was as sweet as honey in my mouth. He said: Son of man, go now to the house of Israel, and speak my word to them (Ez 3:1-4)

NOTES

Chapter One

1. Augustine, *Against the Epistle of Manichaeus Called Fundamental*, no. 6.

2. William Chillingworth, *The Religion of Protestants, A Safe Way to Salvation* (Oxford: L. Lichfield, 1638).

3. *The Documents of Vatican II*, ed. by Walter M. Abbott and Joseph Gallagher, (New York: America Press, 1966). Generally speaking this translation will be followed in the present paper.

4. Willi Marxsen, *The New Testament as the Church's Book* (Philadelphia: Fortress, 1972), chap. 1.

5. Karl Rahner, *Inspiration in the Bible*, 2nd ed. rev. (New York: Herder and Herder, 1964), pp. 49-52.

6. Cf. A.C. Sundberg, "Canon Muratori: A Fourth Century List," *Harvard Theological Review* 66 (1973): 1-41.

7. See R.P.C. Hanson, *Tradition in the Early Church* (Philadelphia: Westminster, 1963), chap. 5.

8. Everett R. Kalin, "The Inspired Community: A Glance at Canon History," *Concordia Theological Monthly* 42 (1971): 541-49.

9. See Rahner, *Inspiration in the Bible*, pp. 70-71.

10. On the reciprocal illumination of the Old and New Testaments see Brevard Childs, *Biblical Theology in Crisis* (Philadelphia: Westminster, 1970); also Roland Murphy, "Christian Understanding of the Old Testament," *Theology Digest* 18 (1970): 330.

11. Rahner, *Inspiration in the Bible*, p. 56.

12. Alec McCowen, quoted in *Washington Post*, Nov. 22, 1978, p.B1.

13. Commenting on *Dei Verbum*, no. 26, Joseph Ratzinger writes: "The universalistic idea of the Preface comes in here again also: 'Let the word of the Lord run and be glorified' (2 Thes 3:1). What has immediately gone before, the readiness to sow the seed of the word of God in scripture generously and fearlessly, even where one is unable to supervise or check what grows out of it, is a full affirmation of the universal meaning and the inner power of the word of God, that does not return without fruit" (Is 55:10) *Commentary on the Documents of Vatican II*, ed. Herbert Vorgrimler (New York: Herder and Herder, 1969), 3:272.

14. Raymond E. Brown, "Difficulties in Using the New Testament in American Catholic Discussions," *Louvain Studies* 6 (1976): 144-58.

15. Rudolf Bultmann, "Is Exegesis without Presuppositions Possible?", *Existence and Faith: Shorter Writings* (New York: Meridian Books, 1960), pp. 293-94.

16. Joseph Ratzinger makes this point in his commentary contained in Vorgrimler, *Commentary*, 3:194. In this connection it is of interest that Vatican Council I had rejected a proposed text to the effect that the scriptures are "vere et proprie verbum Dei scriptum" on the ground that this term should be restricted to the prophetic oracles and the *ipsissima verba* of Jesus himself (cf. N.I. Weyns, "De notione inspirationis biblicae iuxta Concilium Vaticanum," *Angelicum* 30 [1953] 328-30). Yet Vatican II in *Dei Verbum* no. 24 says: "Sacrae autem Scripturae verbum Dei continent et, quia inspiratae, vere verbum Dei sunt." Still it must be recognized that the inspired word of scripture is not the word of God in exactly the same way as if it came directly from the "mouth of God."

17. Cf. Karl Rahner, "Scripture and Tradition," *Theological Investigations*, (Baltimore: Helicon, 1969), 6:98-112; also his article, "Scripture and Tradition," *Encyclopedia of Theology: The Concise 'Sacramentum Mundi'* (New York: Seabury, 1975), pp. 1549-54.

18. Paul Tillich, *Systematic Theology*, (Chicago: University of Chicago, 1951), 1:36-37.

19. Raymond E. Brown, "Hermeneutics," *Jerome Biblical Commentary* (Englewood Cliffs, N.J.: Prentice-Hall, 1968), 71:10.

20. Although the Council wished to avoid taking a position on the controverted question of the *sensus plenior*, it did say that the books of the Old Testament "acquire and show forth their full meaning in the New Testament (in Nova Testamento significationem suam completam acquirunt et ostendunt)," *Dei Verbum* no. 16.

21. The significance of recent philosophical hermeneutics for biblical interpretation is lucidly explored by Sandra M. Schneiders in her article, "Faith, Hermeneutics, and the Literal Sense of Scripture," *Theological Studies* Vol. 39, no. 4 (December 1978): 719-736.

22. Cf. the references and quotations in T.A. Collins and Raymond E. Brown, "Church Pronouncements," *Jerome Biblical Commentary* 72:25.

23. H. Denzinger and A. Schönmetzer, eds., Enchiridion symbolorum definitionum, et declarationum de rebus fidei et morum (Freiburg: Herder, 1963).

24. Pius XII, *DS* 3825.

25. On the ambiguities in the term *authenticus* see Joseph A. Komon-

chak, "*Humanae Vitae* and Its Reception," *Theological Studies* vol. 39 no. 2 (June 1978): p. 223, note 8, and the literature there cited.

26. Raymond E. Brown, "Hermeneutics," *Jerome Biblical Commentary* 71:87.

27. *Ibid.*, 85.

28. George H. Tavard, *Holy Writ or Holy Church: The Crisis of the Protestant Reformation* (New York: Harper and Brothers, 1959), p. 246.

Chapter Three

1. George Martin, *Reading Scripture as the Word of God: Practical Approaches and Attitudes* (Ann Arbor, Mich.: Servant Publications, 1975).

2. See *On Revelation* Article 13.

3. See the link made in Vatican II, *On Revelation*, chap. 3, between inspiration and interpretation.

4. Alois Grillmeier, "Inspiration and Interpretation of Scripture," *Dogmatic Constitution on Divine Revelation* in Herbert Vorgrimler, ed., *Commentary on the Documents of Vatican II* (New York: Herder & Herder, 1967-1968), vol.3, pp. 199-246.

5. *Ibid.*, p. 230.

6. The main sections of Wilhelm Heitmüller's article, "Zum Problem Paulus und Jesus," *Zeitschrift für die Neutestamentliche Wissenschaft* 13 (1912):320-337 are available in English in Wayne A. Meeks, ed., *The Writings of St. Paul*, Norton Critical Edition (New York: Norton, 1972), pp. 308-319.

7. Wilhelm Bousset, *Kyrios Christos*, trans. John E. Steely (Nashville: Abingdon, 1970); Rudolf Bultmann, *Theology of the New Testament*, trans. Kendrick Grobel (New York: Charles Scribner's Sons, Vol. 1, 1951; Vol. 2, 1955); Hans Conzelmann, *History of Primitive Christianity*, trans. John E. Steely (New York: Abingdon, 1973); Reginald Fuller, *The Foundations of New Testament Christology* (New York: Charles Scribner's Sons, 1965); Norman Perrin, *The New Testament, An Introduction* (New York: Harcourt Brace Jovanovich, 1974), chap. 3; Ernst Käsemann, *Essays on New Testament Themes*, trans. W.J. Montague, Studies in Biblical Theology, (London: SCM, 1964), p.63-107,; Ernst Käsemann, *New Testament Questions of Today*, (Philadelphia: Fortress, 1969), pp. 236-51.

8. On the anti-Jewish bias, see Charlotte Klein, *Anti-Judaism in Christian Theology*, trans. Edward Quinn (Philadelphia: Fortress, 1977), and E.P. Sanders, *Paul and Palestinian Judaism* (Philadelphia: Fortress, 1977).

9. Rudolf Bultmann, *The Gospel of John: A Commentary*, trans. G.R. Beasley-Murray et. al. (Philadelphia: Westminster, 1971). See the excellent critique by Nils A. Dahl, "Rudolf Bultmann's *Theology of the New Testament*," in his *The Crucified Messiah* (Minneapolis: Augsburg, 1974), pp. 90-128, notes pp. 175-177.

10. Walter Bauer, *Orthodoxy and Heresy in Earliest Christianity*, ed. Robert A. Kraft and Gerhard Krodel (Philadelphia: Fortress, 1971).

11. Nils A. Dahl, *Das Volk Gottes* (Darmstadt: Wissenschaftliche Buchgesellschaft, 1963 reprint).

12. For a readable reconstruction, which I find more plausible than the predominant ones, see Stephen Neill's *Jesus Through Many Eyes* (Philadelphia: Fortress, 1976), chap. 2. An excellent in-depth treatment is James D.G. Dunn, *Unity and Diversity in the New Testament: An Inquiry into the Character of Earliest Christianity* (Philadelphia: Westminster, 1977), written as an alternative to Bauer and continuation and updating of the earlier fine work by C.F.D. Moule, *The Birth of the New Testament*, 2nd rev. ed., Black's New Testament Commentaries, (London: Black, 1962, 1966) companion vol. 1. For a critique of other theories of origins which is similar to mine, see C.F.D. Moule, *The Origin of Christology* (New York: Cambridge, 1977), especially pp. 1-10.

13. Hans Schürmann, *Jesu Ureigener Tod*, 2nd rev. ed. (Freiburg: Herder, 1975), especially pp. 56-96.

14. A different perspective, with more stress on Mark's *creative* role in his passion narrative, is given by John R. Donahue, *Are You the Christ? The Trial Narrative in the Gospel of Mark*, SBL Dissertation Series, 10 (Missoula, Mont.: Scholars Press, 1973).

15. James D.G. Dunn, *Jesus and the Spirit: A Study of the Religious and Charismatic Experience of Jesus and the First Christians as Reflected in the New Testament* (Philadelphia: Westminster, 1975).

16. Willi Marxsen, *The Resurrection of Jesus of Nazareth*, trans. Margaret Kohl (Philadelphia: Fortress, 1970).

17. For an excellent, balanced treatment that discusses all the important views, see Raymond E. Brown, *The Virginal Conception and Bodily Resurrection of Jesus* (New York: Paulist, 1973), chap. 2. A simplified but still good treatment is Edward J. Ciuba's *Who Do You Say That I Am?* (New York: Alba, 1974), chap. 8.

18. For provocative suggestions about wandering missionaries and local communities, even if not well argued, see Gerd Theissen, *Sociology of Early Palestinian Christianity*, trans. John Bowden (Philadelphia: Fortress, 1977). See also the popular but careful treatment by Abraham Malherbe, "House Churches and Their Problems," in his *Social Aspects of Early Christianity*, Rockwell Lectures, Rice University (Baton Rouge: Louisiana State University Press, 1977).

19. E.g., in Hans Küng, *The Church* (New York: Sheed and Ward, 1967).

20. See the excellent treatment in Arthur Darby Nock, *Conversion* (London: Oxford University Press, 1933).

21. Cf. Bousset, *Kyrios Christos*.

22. Nils A. Dahl, "The Particularity of the Pauline Epistles as a Problem in the Ancient Church," in *Neotestamentica et Patristica. Freundesgabe O. Cullmann*, Supplements to Novum Testamentum, 6 (Leiden: Brill, 1962), pp. 261-271.

23. A convenient treatment of this problem is found in K. Koch, "Pseudonymous Writing," *Interpreter's Dictionary of the Bible, Supplementary Volume*, ed. Keith R. Crim et. al. (Nashville: Abingdon, 1976), pp. 712-714.

24. Raymond E. Brown, *Jerome Biblical Commentary* (Englewood Cliffs, N.J.: Prentice Hall, 1968) 67:88-89.

25. *Ibid.*, 87; *Jerome Biblical Commentary*, 72:25.

26. Cf. *Jerome Biblical Commentary*, 64:83.

27. See the treatment of the canon in any good commentary or New Testament introduction.

Chapter Four

1. A case in point is the recent study by Anthony Kosnik et al., *Human Sexuality: New Directions in American Catholic Thought* (New York: Paulist Press, 1977), which, despite its merits, has come under serious criticism from several sources for its deficiencies in handling the biblical material.

2. "Though...within institutions of theological learning and education the historical method of reading enjoys a dominant position, there is much dissatisfaction about that position from the side of theology itself. It is repeatedly asked whether a historical study of the Bible can prove adequate for religious needs. How does one get from what the

text meant to what it now means? Can the biblical scholar, along with the results of his historical research, also give some direction to the theologian about the implications of this for religion in the present time? — and often, it seems, he cannot." J.A. Barr, "Reading the Bible as Literature," *Bulletin of the John Rylands University Library of Manchester* 56 (1973-74):20.

3. Cf. *Dei Verbum, 11-12; Divino Afflante Spiritu,* 23. The same may be said of the Biblical Commission's *Instructio de Historica Evangeliorum Veritate* of April 21, 1964.

4. Cf. Gerhard Maier, *The End of the Historical Critical Method* (St. Louis: Concordia Publishing House, 1977).

5. A survey of the situation is given in Everard C. Johnston's "From an Author-Oriented to a Text-Oriented Hermeneutic: Implications of Paul Ricoeur's Hermeneutical Theory for the Interpretation of the New Testament," (Ph.D. diss., Louvain, 1977), 1-23, 171. See also Peter Stuhlmacher, *Historical Criticism and Theological Interpretation of Scripture* (Philadelphia: Fortress Press, 1977).

6. Walter Wink, *The Bible in Human Transformation: Toward a New Paradigm for Biblical Study* (Philadelphia: Fortress Press, 1973), p. 1.

7. Wink, *The Bible,* p. 2.

8. *Ibid.,* p. 3.

9. *Ibid.,* pp. 10-11.

10. Krister Stendahl, "Rooted in the Communities of Faith: A Reaffirmation of a Learned Ministry," *Theological Education* 13 (1977):63.

11. Wink, *The Bible,* p. 12.

12. Bultmann himself would hardly have called this a "salvage" operation, for he was ideologically committed to the fact that the negative results of historical criticism were actually a triumph for the Christian faith, which, like justification by faith without works, now found itself liberated from dependence on historical foundations in order to encounter God in the preached word. Rudolph Bultmann, *Kerygma and Myth,* ed. Hans W. Bartsch (New York: Harper Torchbooks, 1961), pp. 210-211.

13. Thomas S. Kuhn, *The Structure of Scientific Revolutions* (Chicago: University of Chicago Press, 1970), p. 5.

14. Norman Perrin, "The Modern Interpretation of the Parables of Jesus and the Problem of Hermeneutics," *Interpretation* 25 (1971):145.

15. Norman Perrin dedicated his last work to Amos Wilder and Paul Ricoeur, "who taught me to look at the problem of hermeneutics in new

ways." *Jesus and the Language of the Kingdom: Symbol and Metaphor in New Testament Interpretation* (Philadelphia: Fortress Press, 1976), p. v.

16. Paul Ricoeur especially disagrees with the tenet of structuralist philosophy, according to which the text has only sense but no reference (i.e., the world of the text). See Johnston, *Text-Oriented Hermeneutic*, pp. 101, 106.

17. Daniel Patte, *What is Structural Exegesis?* (Philadelphia: Fortress Press, 1976), p. 1.

18. Patte, *Structural Exegesis*, pp. 24-25.

19. Paul Ricoeur, *Interpretation Theory: Discourse and the Surplus of Meaning* (Fort Worth: Texas Christian University Press, 1976), pp. 92-94.

20. The aim of interpretation, in Schleiermacher's view, is "die Rede zuerst so gut und dann besser zu verstehen als ihr Urheber." Friedrich E. Schleiermacher, *Hermeneutik* (Heidelberg: Winter, Universitatsverlag, 1959), 87. Ernesti, however, already limited this as the intention understood only from the author's words. Hans W. Frei, *The Eclipse of Biblical Narrative: A Study in Eighteenth and Nineteenth Century Hermeneutics* (New Haven: Yale University Press, 1974), p. 252.

21. Ricoeur, *Interpretation Theory*, p. 75-76.

22. Cf. Johnston, *Text-Oriented Hermeneutic*, pp. 63-76, especially p. 75.

23. *Ibid.*, p. 133.

24. See note 5 above.

25. Ricoeur, *Interpretation Theory*, p. 93.

26. *Ibid.*

27. Dominic Crossan, *The Dark Interval: Towards a Theology of Story* (Niles, Ill.: Argus Communications, 1975), p. 102.

28. Bernard Lonergan, *Method in Theology* (New York: Herder & Herder, 1972), pp. 161-162.

29. Ricoeur, *Interpretation Theory*, pp. 94-95.

30. Of course the point is made repeatedly in the rabbinic tradition. "The one who learns in order not to do would better have not been created," *Sipra Behuqqotai Parasha* 1.5 to Lv 26:3, quoted in E.P. Sanders, *Paul and Palestinian Judaism* (London: SCM Press, 1977), p. 107.

31. David Lochhead, "Hermeneutics and Ideology," *The Ecumenist* 15 (1977): 83-84.

32. Paul Ricoeur, *Freud and Philosophy* (New Haven: Yale University Press, 1970), 419-458. Pope Paul VI echoed the same concern in an

address to exegetes in 1970: "In every interpretative process, and with greater reason when it is a matter of God's word, the person of the interpreter is not outside of the process itself, but is involved in it, brought into question, with all his being. God's word is 'lively and powerful' (Heb 4:12) and 'able to build up and give an inheritance among the sanctified' (Acts 20:32). If this is so, then, in order to get into serious contact with it and consider it for what it really is: God's word which works 'in those who believe' (cf. 1 Thes 2:13), it is necessary to enter into the dialogue which it means to conduct in an authoritative fashion with every man." *Acta Apostolicae Sedis* 62 (1970): 615-619. English ed. of *l'Osservatore Romano*, (October 8, 1970):2.

33. Juan-Luis Segundo, *The Liberation of Theology* (New York: Orbis, 1976), p. 9. I am grateful to my friend and colleague, Francis Martin, for calling this text to my attention.

34. Stuhlmacher, *Historical Criticism*, pp. 84-91.

35. Cf. Lonergan, *Method*, p. 163.

36. Cf. Richard E. Palmer, *Hermeneutics: Interpretation Theory in Schleiermacher, Dilthey, Heidegger, and Gadamer* (Evanston: Northwestern University Press, 1969), pp. 235-237.

Chapter Five

1. Richard Rohr, "The Bible," *Catholic Charismatic*, vol. 2 no. 2 (June/July, 1977):5.

2. The proceedings for the subcommittee on the use of scripture in teaching were summarized by George Martin, publisher for Servant Publications.

3. Three introductory programs successfully initiate people into the charismatic experience: (1.) *The Life in the Spirit Seminars Team Manual*, 4th ed. rev. (Ann Arbor, Mich.: Servant Books, 1973, 1979); *The Life in the Spirit Seminars Team Manual*, Catholic ed. (Ann Arbor, Mich.: Servant Books, 1979); (2.)Sr. Phillip Marie Burle and Sr. Sharon Ann Plankenhorn, *You Will Receive Power* (Pecos, N. Mex.: Dove Publications, 1977); (3.)Anthony Cushing and Daniel Thomson, *Living Christian Community* (Ramsey, N.J.: Paulist Press, 1978). All three offer specialized team manuals. The regular edition of *The Life in the Spirit Seminars* is ecumenical in thrust and stresses the fundamentals of Christianity whereas *You Will Receive Power*, *Living Christian Community*, and the Catholic edition of *The Life in the Spirit Seminars*

take into consideration sacramental theology and a Catholic ecclessiology. *Living Christian Community* is the new team manual for the four works previously entitled *Friendship with Jesus*, *Worshipping Community*, *Freedom and Healing*, and *Called to Service* (New York: Paulist Press, 1976).

4. Father George Montague originally presented this text to the Catholic Biblical Association of America in his presidential address. Therefore, his remarks were initially addressed to the specialized audience of professional theologians and then later shared in the context of this symposium.

5. The proceedings for the subcommittee on the directive use of scripture were summarized by William S. O'Brien, liaison for the Archdiocese of Newark and member of the Community of God's Love, Rutherford, New Jersey.

6. The proceedings for the subcommittee on the use of scripture for prayer and sanctification were summarized by Donald Gelpi, distinguished author and professor at the Jesuit School of Theology, Berkeley, California.

7. This theme is further developed in Donald Gelpi, *Charism and Sacrament: A Theology of Christian Conversion* (New York: Paulist Press, 1976), especially chap. 2, which particularly develops the specific moral obligations of those who follow Jesus and are transformed by the Spirit.